Aberdour Golf Club

THE FIRST HUNDRED YEARS

Jack Bald

Aberdour Golf Club 1896-1996

ISBN 0 9531670 0 3

A catalogue record for this book is available from the British Library.

Printed in Scotland by Sprint Repro, Dunfermline. Published by Aberdour Golf Club, Seaside Place, Aberdour KY3 0TX, Fife

CONTENTS

Note:

Details given in Appendices 3, 4 and 5 were taken from the Club Trophies

FOREWORD _____

At Aberdour Golf Club we have now completed our first Centenary. What better time to record the history of the Club to date?

The founding fathers of the Club, including my great

grandfather, the Club's first Secretary, would little realise the great pleasure their action was to give to so many golfers during the following generations.

Few can deny that Aberdour Golf Club is located in an idyllic setting with panoramic views of the Forth Estuary. The course, whilst relatively short, presents a challenge on every occasion of play.

Aberdour Golf Club is greatly indebted to Jack Bald for undertaking the task of researching the history of the Club and preparing this book. It is a story well worth telling and the finished product is the result of years of research and many hours delving in the Club records.

I am delighted to introduce this illustrated story of Aberdour Golf Club and commend it to you.

With good wishes,

Willie Crowe

Captain, Aberdour Golf Club

INTRODUCTION
AND ACKNOWLEDGEMENTS _____

Just over five years ago and with the Club's Centenary in mind, the Council considered that a book should be written to record the first hundred years of the Club's existence. As a result of this decision I was approached and invited to undertake the work.

Despite a few setbacks along the way, it turned out to be a most pleasant and interesting exercise. Because of the lack of detailed early Club records, the book tends to concentrate on the latter half of the century. Nevertheless, I hope it will give new members some idea of how Aberdour Golf Club developed over the years and for older members revive happy memories.

I offer my sincerest thanks to the many who contributed to the compilation of the history of the Club and I include those members who took the trouble to look out old photographs, newspaper cuttings relating to Club events, those who volunteered and verified information and the leading Club players who completed profiles.

I am particularly grateful to Mrs Pat Hughes who found time, despite all her other duties, to type the first draft of the narrative along with the long lists of Trophy winners and to Bill Allan for providing me with a great deal of background information and for his contribution to the article on the next hundred years.

Four other people deserve a special word of thanks: Bob Pearston, Chairman of the Centenary Committee; Graham Milne and David Ritchie, Centenary Committee members, who devoted so much of their spare time to editing, re-drafting and putting together the final touches to the book; and Mrs May Stewart whose help and advice proved invaluable in setting out the book ready for the printers. Her patience and understanding were very much appreciated, as passages were inserted or modified right up to the last minute and to May I give my sincerest thanks.

Jack Bald, July 1997

THE EARLY YEARS

Towards the end of the 19th Century, the game of golf was gaining in popularity and many of the towns and villages along the Fife coast were keen to have a golf course for the use of both locals and summer visitors. A local committee had been set up in Aberdour, probably as early as 1893, to search for ground suitable for development as a golf course. Initially their efforts to find a site were unsuccessful but in 1896 they were rewarded by obtaining a 3 year lease on 40 to 50 acres of pastureland on the farm of Couston on the western outskirts of the village. A yearly rent of £50 was to be paid, with the farmer retaining the right to graze sheep over the course.

Although the location and the site were far from ideal it was decided to proceed with the project and a Bazaar was held to raise some finance to fund the construction of the new golf course. The amount raised was in the order of £300 which was a substantial sum in the 1890s and quite sufficient to enable the project to be carried out.

A club was formed, members were enrolled and the first annual meeting of the club was held in the Woodside Hall on 22nd June 1896. The Rev W H Gray was elected Captain of the Club and remained so throughout the existence of the Club at Couston. Membership in the first year of the club stood at 62 gentlemen, 16 ladies and 3 youths.

Rev W H Gray

With the aid of Willie Park of Musselburgh, a nine hole course was laid out on a triangular strip of ground on the south side of the Inverkeithing road from the present roundabout west to the Chesters cottages (known locally as the Four Lums). Because the turf was of such good quality, it was decided that there would be no need to completely re-lay the new greens and that fairways would soon be brought up to standard by normal cutting and regular play. As a result, play would be possible almost immediately.

Detailed plans of the course layout are no longer in existence but the diagram on the following page is reasonably accurate. It was drawn from information obtained from a number of sources including the local newspaper, the Dunfermline Journal. At a total of 3105 yards in length for the nine holes, the course was fairly long, especially as most players had only a few clubs, such as a driver, brassie, cleek, mashie and putter. The longest hole was the seventh which measured 410 yards with only two holes, the fifth and the eighth, under 300 yards.

The first recorded course record was set in the summer of 1897 when a Willie Binnie of Kinghorn, playing in a foursome which included Matthew Brown, the first Aberdour professional, returned a score of 80 for eighteen holes.

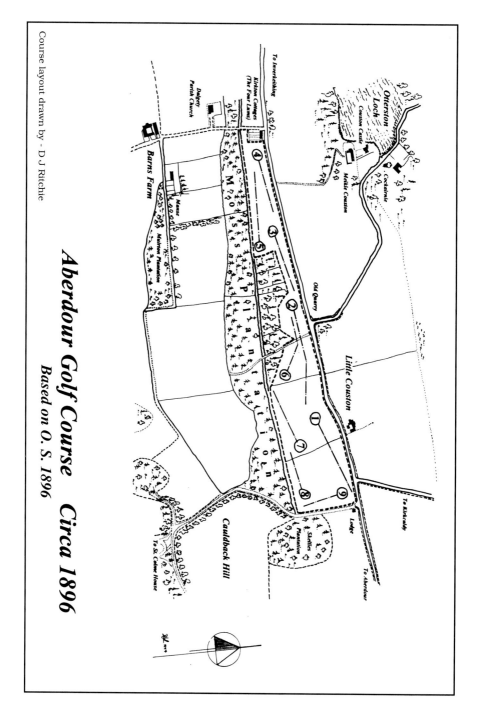

Aberdour Golf Course Circa 1896

Based on O. S. 1896

Course layout drawn by - D J Ritchie

An official ceremony to mark the opening of the course was not held until 1897. A marquee was erected on the course, a camera set up and a photograph taken of the principal guests. This photograph is shown below.

One amusing incident from those early years was remembered by Walter Crow, who as a young boy attended the opening ceremony in 1897. During play in a competition a player struck a sheep with his approach shot to the first hole, the ball lodging in its fleece. The sheep took fright and as it bolted across the green, the ball dropped from the sheep's back and landed close to the hole. The committee, when asked to give a decision on the incident, concluded that the ball was still in flight and should be played where it had come to rest without penalty.

After a few years of play on the new course, during which time the fairways and greens were greatly improved, the Club suffered what at that time was probably a major set-back. The lease of the ground at Couston was not renewed and once again the members faced a search for suitable ground. During this time the club was not allowed to become defunct and members continued playing over Burntisland Golf Course until finally an approach to the Factor for the Earl of Moray for ground more adjacent to the sea was successful.

The Club was offered Bellhouse Park to the west of Seaside Place on condition that -

fairway would be at least 50 yards from the Avenue leading to Donibristle House

and

no player would be allowed access to the Avenue to search for a lost golf ball.

By 1905 a nine hole golf course had been laid out and was ready for play. The formal opening by the Earl of Moray took place on Monday 10 April 1905. At the ceremony, which took place close to the first tee, the Earl was presented with a silver mounted driver and invited to drive the first ball. His Lordship admitted he was not an expert but nevertheless he agreed to the request. Unfortunately his first and second attempts to hit the ball were unsuccessful but his third shot resulted in a good drive. The first Clubhouse at Seaside Place is shown in the photograph below and was situated immediately to the left of the entrance to the course.

From this formal opening in 1905 to the start of the First World War, the club made steady progress. By 1912 membership had increased, particularly on the ladies' side, to 88 men, 94 ladies and 4 youths, and in that same year work was started on an 18 hole layout. However, the war clouds were gathering and although 1914 saw the formal opening of the first 18 hole course, war was imminent and the next 4 or 5 years saw falling membership and low activity in the club.

By early 1919 the war was over, the young men of the village who had served with the Armed Forces were returning and interest in the game of golf was regenerated. This year was marked by the addition of two new cups to the trophy list and which are now amongst the oldest in the Club. The first was the Victory Cup which was purchased by the Club to mark the ending of the war and to give some recognition to those who had served in the Forces and shown such devotion to their country. The second trophy was presented to the Club in November by the Officers of the Grand Fleet in recognition of their being allowed to play over the course during the war. The silver cup to be called The Grand Fleet Cup was presented to the Club Captain Rev J Brown by Admiral Sir Arthur Liveson. A suggestion was made that the competition be played as near as possible to the date of the Battle of Jutland which took place on 30 May 1916.

THE TWENTIES AND THIRTIES

In a short history of the Club it is impossible to record every item of interest in a twenty year period. However, from conversations with members past and present it was obvious this was a very happy time for them. As the country recovered after the First World War, membership steadily increased and, in fact, by 1929 it became necessary to restrict membership to 175 men, 100 ladies and 25 youths.

There had been little change in the 18 hole course layout since it was opened but in 1928 some course reconstruction was undertaken and two new holes were laid out, one of which is remembered happily, or otherwise, by anyone who has played golf over the Aberdour course. This was the construction of the tee and green of our present second hole (Firs) which is arguably the most picturesque hole in Fife. Present day members might also like to know that the large hollow on the third fairway (Ainsley's Pier), which on medal days catches many of our drives, was not a natural hazard but was created originally in 1929 when 600-700 tons of sand were extracted and used to fill many of the bunkers on the Course.

The cottage bungalow-type Clubhouse shown in the photograph replaced the original Clubhouse, probably in the early 1920's and with a number of alterations and extensions served members until 1965 when the new and present Clubhouse was built. The tee which can be seen in the foreground of the Clubhouse photograph was the par 4 (Kinniker) first hole (now our present 17th).

Club ties and badges are quite common in most Golf Clubs but members may not be aware that, in 1927, official club colours were adopted by Aberdour. These consisted of a scarlet blazer with a monogram badge in white silk thread embracing the initials AGC. Blazers had plain buttons in silver and were available from R W Forsyth, Princes Street, Edinburgh at a cost of two guineas. No doubt several of these blazers were purchased over the years but so far none have been traced and no one has any recollection of their existence. However, one of the earliest issues of Club badges turned up in 1982. It was discovered in a Perth, Western Australia, antique shop by a Mrs Tanner. She donated the silver plated badge, with Aberdour Golf Club in white and numbered 89, to the Club and it is on display in the Trophy Cabinet. It is understood to date from around 1910. In return the Club presented Mrs Tanner's Club in Western Australia, Waterside Workers' Social Club whose members play over Lakes Hotel Golf Course in Hilton, with a small trophy.

They say it never rains on the golf course, well in 1933 and 1934 this was true. Aberdour was faced with severe drought conditions and the course suffered badly. Green staff were forced to work night shifts watering greens to prevent the serious consequences of prolonged baking. As a result, early as 1934 the Council was giving serious consideration to either moving to another site or opening a second course which had a natural supply of water on hand. Two sites were considered, Hillside Estate and Aberdour House Estate, both of which border the Dour Burn. In the event neither project got off the ground although preliminary discussions did take place.

Three new Club competitions started during this 20 year period and are still running today, namely, the Moubray Cup presented by Admiral and Major Moubray in 1928, the Cameron Cup in 1929 and the New Year's Day competition in 1923. The prize for the last was the same as it is today, a bottle of whisky, which in 1923 cost 12/6d and today costs in the region of £13.50.

Some alterations to the format of certain competitions also took place. In 1935 the Hewitt Medal was changed to its present format, the Victory Cup became a foursomes competition and for the first time the Challenge Cup was contested over two rounds. In that same year Ian Moyes set a course record of 63.

The highlight of the 1936 season was an exhibition match in aid of the Aberdour and District Nursing Association which was held over the Aberdour Course on Saturday 13 June 1936. A large crowd turned out to watch Hector Thomson, the British Amateur Champion, and Jack McLean (Gleneagles) play fourball matches with two Aberdour members, R L Johnstone and R F Cuthill, the Club Champion.

In the afternoon game, McLean and Cuthill triumphed over Thomson and Johnstone by 5 and 3, Thomson being unable to repeat his form of the previous evening when he set a course record of 60. The individual afternoon scores were Thomson 67, McLean 63, Cuthill 65 and Johnstone

The Exhibition Match - 1936

66. However the tables were turned in the evening game when Thomson and Johnstone won by 4 and 2. The spectators were treated to some very fine golf with 3 players, Thomson, McLean and Johnstone all shooting 61's and Cuthill a 65. McLean's round was particularly good as he ran up a 6 at the 8th (Downings) but was still out in 29.

The day had been a great success with Thomson and McLean being presented with Silver Quaichs as souvenirs of the occasion and the Nursing Association with a handsome cheque.

Many of our present day members are also members of the Bowling Club and they may be interested to know that in 1937 the Dunfermline District Council handed over the running of both the putting and bowling greens to the Golf Club. This decision followed complaints about the poor condition of the greens. Moray Estate agreed to transfer the lease to the Golf Club. The greens were then maintained by the Golf Course greenkeeping staff. In order to further improve facilities, the Golf Club Council also decided to purchase 20 pairs of new bowls at a cost of one pound and eight pence (£1/0/8d) a pair. In addition, the Golf Club decided to construct two tennis courts at the end of the Public Park and to provide tennis equipment for hire by the general public. A full-time attendant was provided for the summer season and the greens and courts were maintained on a regular basis. These arrangements remained for over 20 years. Eventually the Bowling and Tennis Clubs decided they would prefer to maintain and run their own affairs and after consultation with the Golf Club, the transfer of the leases to the respective Clubs was agreed to by the Moray Estates.

The Club history would not be complete without a mention of the number one social event of those years. Undoubtedly, during this period and immediately after the Second World War, the highlight of the Club social calendar and indeed of the village, was the Golf Club Dinner Dance which was held annually, usually in the Woodside Hotel. However, because of the popularity of the inaugural function in 1927 and the huge demand for tickets for this event, the second Dinner in 1928 was held in the Aberdour Palais de Danse. The "Palais" was situated behind the Woodside Hotel and the building is still in use although it ceased to be a dance hall many years ago.

As can be seen from the photograph, dinner jacket and evening dress were mandatory in those early years. Menus were printed for the occasion and over the years the assembled company were entertained by some excellent guest speakers. For example, in 1938, the toast to the Club was proposed by the Secretary of the R&A.

The Golf Dinner was always the last official duty of the retiring Captain

who made a farewell speech before his wife presented the annual trophies. In those days junior members and prize winners not attending the dinner waited in the hotel corridor until their name was called by the Head Waiter. Some members may remember waiting nervously in the wings prior to making the long walk to the top table to receive their trophy.

After the prize-giving, the dinner tables were cleared to make way for the dancing. During this lull in proceedings, the time was used not only to replenish drinks, but to get dance cards filled, a popular custom of the times which has now totally disappeared. The evening usually finished at 2am with a hot bovril drink prior to departure. Many members and their wives then made their way to the railway station to catch a special train, arranged by the Council, to convey them to Edinburgh. This arrangement may seem strange to many of our present day members but for many years a very large proportion of the membership were permanently resident in Edinburgh.

Finally, one small interesting item to round off this period in the Club's history. A Council decision in 1931 allowed caddies at Aberdour for the first time at a charge of one shilling and tuppence per round - this included one penny to the Club and one penny to the starter. For those unfamiliar with old money this is roughly equivalent to 6p today.

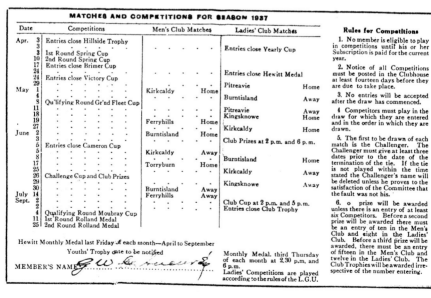

Fixture Card for 1937

At the outbreak of war in 1939 it soon became apparent that the Golf Club would have to be prepared to adapt to a rapidly changing situation. It was initially rumoured that most of the course would be required for agricultural purposes in order to produce much needed foodstuffs. However, it was soon announced that the military would be setting up defensive gun emplacements on the golf course in an area adjacent to the sea. Very soon after this announcement construction started and immediately the club lost the use of three holes, the 16th (Pavilion), 17th (Kinniker) and 18th (Roundel). In addition, the trees in the Roundel were cut down. By July 1940 construction was well under way and the Clubhouse had been requisitioned by the Army. Two huts were erected in the trees at the dogleg to the present 16th (Pavilion) hole to serve as a Clubhouse and professional's shop. Coiled barbed wire was installed from the wall at the Manse running up the hill to the corner of the Kinniker Wood next to the 5th (Oxcar) tee. The Club was now left with a ten hole course, the first hole being the present 13th (Downings) and the 10th hole the present 15th (Woodside). For 18 hole competitions members played the first 9 holes twice. Competitions were usually on Saturday afternoons over 18 holes which for the two nines produced a par of 70. Entrance to the course was via the gate at the back of the tennis courts.

Wartime conditions meant that no full time employees could be used as greenkeeping staff and the course was therefore maintained using part-time staff under the direction of the green convener. Bunkers and rough were never raked or cut and these hazards eventually became formidable. Golf balls eventually became very scarce and consequently the 5 minute search rule for a ball lost in the rough was stretched to the extreme. Golf tees were also very scarce and most players used sand provided in the Tee Boxes to make a tee. As there was no Sunday golf permitted, a common Sunday occupation for the youths of the village was searching the rough for valuable balls.

The organisation and running of the Golf Club throughout the war years fell mainly on the shoulders of three men, Tom Nisbet (Secretary), Cathol Kerr (Treasurer) and Johnny Bald (Match Secretary). They had to fit these duties on top of their normal jobs and also being members of Voluntary Services such as the Home Guard and ARP.

Another change which had a minor effect on the Golf Club and Village life during the war was the arrival of the Polish Army. By 1943 the Royal Artillery had served its function of defending the approaches to the Forth Bridge and Rosyth Naval Dockyard. The RA therefore pulled out of the Golf Course camp and was replaced by detachments of the Polish Army based in this country. The Polish Officers still continued to use the Clubhouse as their mess and during their stay constructed three coloured concrete emblems on the banking close to the present 17th (Kinniker) tee. One emblem was a map of Scotland, the second the Polish Eagle and

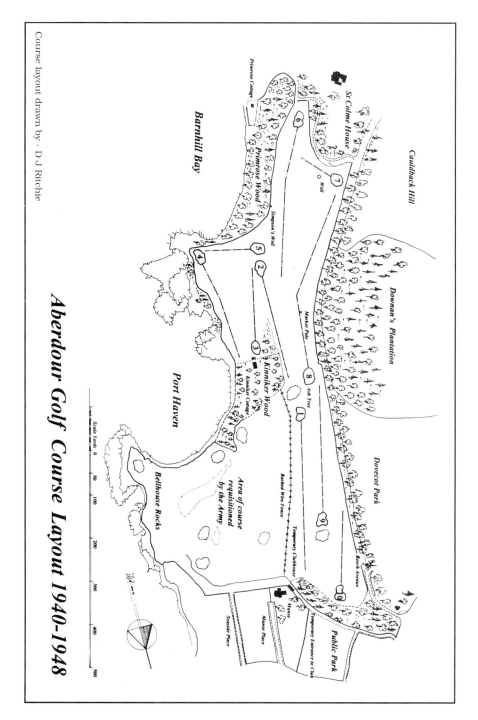

Aberdour Golf Course Layout 1940-1948

Course layout drawn by - D J Ritchie

Cauldback Hill

St Colme House

Primrose Cottage

Barnhill Bay

Primrose Wood

Simpson's Well

Downan's Plantation

Marker Pole

Kinniker Wood

Kinniker Cottage

Ash Tree

Dovecot Park

Port Haven

Bellhouse Rocks

Area of course
requisitioned
by the Army

Barbed Wire Fence

Temporary Clubhouse

Beech Avenue

Manse

Manse Place

Seaside Place

Public Park

Temporary Entrance to Club

Well

Scale Yards   0   50   100   200   300   400   500

12

the third was their Regimental emblem. Unfortunately these records of the past fell into disrepair and disappeared but were subsequently unearthed, as later described by Bill Cochrane.

After the cessation of hostilities in 1945, the main pre-occupation of the Golf Club was obviously to return to a full 18 hole course.

Income had been low for some time and as a result funds were not exactly plentiful. The compensatory rent paid by the Military amounted to only £44/5/- a year and any further compensation from the War Department was minimal. The Abstract of Accounts and Balance for the year ending 30 November 1945 are reproduced on pages 15 and 16 and are indicative of some of the problems to be overcome in the post-war years.

The biggest problem with returning the course to the same layout as in pre-war years was the removal of the reinforced concrete gun emplacements in the area where the present Clubhouse is situated. Removal of these and various other military buildings was obviously going to be a major and costly civil engineering task. Various possibilities were discussed at the time with the Moray Estates and the War Department including the relocation to the Hillside Estate or the extension of the course into the area known as Dovecot Park. However, the Golf Club was determined to retain its image as a seaside course with the Bellhouse Rock as part of its character and the other options were rejected.

Gradually over the period 1946 to 1948 progress was made towards restoring the former course. The Polish Army eventually departed in 1947, the Clubhouse being returned to the Club in September of that year. The official release of the course by the War Department was on 23 February 1948. It is interesting to note that as the demolition of the Army quarters got under way an approach was made to the Golf Club for permission to recover the old bricks from the buildings being demolished. Permission was granted and for many painstaking months thousands of bricks were recovered by one man and used in the construction of a bungalow at the West End of the village.

re-opening of Course 1948

Aberdour Golf Club.

THE ANNUAL GENERAL MEETING of the ABERDOUR GOLF CLUB will be held in the WOODSIDE HOTEL, Aberdour, on SATURDAY, 24th FEBRUARY 1945, at 3 p.m.

AGENDA.

Minutes.
Council's Report.
Audited Accounts.
Honoraria.
Election of Members of Council.

OFFICE-BEARERS due to retire:—

Captain	...	Mr J. W. W. Kemp, F.S.I.
Vice-Captain	...	Mr W. E. Crowe.
Secretary	...	Mr T. H. M. Nisbet.
Treasurer	...	Mr C. J. Kerr.

MEMBERS due to retire:—

Messrs Jas. B. Bald, John Bald, Junr., Geo. Kelley, W. F. Lorimer, S. E. Mosby, W. Nicholson, E. B. C. Scott, W. M. Thomson.

Appointment of Auditor.
Any other competent business.

T. H. M. NISBET,
Secretary.

2 Viewforth Terrace,
Aberdour,
January 1945.

---

2. BOWLING AND PUTTING GREENS AND TENNIS COURTS.

1943. INCOME.

BALANCE FROM LAST ACCOUNT	£31 16 0	
Less—Income Tax (Sch. D)	1 10 0	
	£30 6 0	£36 9 7
BOWLING GREEN:—		
74 Members	£14 16 0	
3588 Games at 2d	29 18 0	
1349 Games at 4d	22 9 8	
Locker Rents	2 18 0	
	70 1 8	71 0 8
PUTTING GREEN:—		
4023 Rounds at 1d	£16 15 3	
2709 Rounds at 2d	22 11 6	
	39 6 9	55 9 3
TENNIS COURTS:—		
216 Games at 1/-	£10 16 0	
542 Hires at 2d	4 10 4	
	15 6 4	10 4 0
		£173 3 6

1943. EXPENDITURE.

ORDINARY EXPENDITURE:—		
Upkeep of Greens and Courts	£0 10 6	
Rent, Taxes and Insurance	13 4 9	
Tickets	13 1 2	
Repairs and Renewals	0 3 0	
Management	6 6 0	
Wages	92 17 0	
Interest	14 8 0	
		£140 10 5
BALANCE carried forward		14 10 4
		£155 0 9

£141 7 6
31 16 0
£173 3 6
£155 0 9

BALANCE SHEET as at 30th November 1944.

LIABILITIES.

1943.		
£51 16 0	1. SUNDRY CREDITORS	£34 10 4
	2. BANK:—	
	Current A/c—Dr.... £11 9 1	
	Less Savings A/c—Cr. 2 17 5	9 1 8
	3. BALANCE AT CREDIT at 30th November 1943 ...£174 15 3	
	Deduct—Deficit for year ... 75 2 8	1099 12 7
		£1226 11 3

ASSETS.

1943.		
	1. CLUBHOUSE:— Value at 30th November 1943 £185 0 0	£185 0 0
	2. CLUBHOUSE FURNISHINGS:— Value at 30th November 1943 ...£ 14 0 0	
	Less—Depreciation 4 0 0	10 0 0
	3. TENNIS COURTS ... 360 0 0	360 0 0
	4. INVESTMENTS AT COST:—	
	3½% War Loan ...£105 5 3	
	National Savings Certificates 250 8 0	
	Halifax Building Society 229 5 8	584 18 11
	5. CASH ON HAND	3 5 8
		£1226 11 3

EDINBURGH, *16th January 1945.*—I have examined and audited the Accounts of the Aberdour Golf Club for the year ended 30th November, 1944, of which the foregoing are Abstracts. I have obtained all the information and explanations which I have required, and in my opinion the Balance Sheet is properly drawn up so as to exhibit a true and correct view of the state of the Club's affairs as at 30th November, 1944, according to the best of my information and the explanations given to me and as shown by the Books of the Club.

(Signed) HELEN M. SOMERVILLE, C.A.

EDINBURGH, 16th January 1945.

15

R. K. LINDSAY & CO., DUNFERMLINE

ABERDOUR GOLF CLUB.

Minutes of Extraordinary General Meeting of Aberdour Golf Club held in Woodside Hotel, Aberdour, on Saturday, 24th February, 1944, at 3 p.m.

Only 13 members being present, the prescribed quorum was not obtained, and the meeting was consequently designated an Extraordinary General Meeting, and the business conducted accordingly.

The Minutes of the previous Extraordinary General Meeting, which had been printed and circulated, were again read and adopted.

The Council's Report as printed was adopted.

The Annual Accounts and Balance Sheet were adopted.

Certain Honoraria were granted.

The following Office-Bearers were elected for the year :—

Captain—Mr J. W. W. Kemp, F.S.I.

Vice-Captain—Mr W. E. Crowe.

Secretary—Mr T. H. M. Nisbet.

Treasurer—Mr C. J. Kerr.

Members of Council—

Messrs Jas. B. Bald, John Bald, Junr., Geo. Kelley, W. F. Lorimer, S. E. Mosby, W. Nicholson, E. B. C. Scott, and W. M. Thomson.

Miss Helen M. Somerville, C.A., was re-appointed Auditor.

REPORT by the Council for the Year ended 30th November, 1944.

ACCOUNTS.—The ban imposed on this area last summer had an adverse effect on the Club, and this is reflected in the accounts.

There is a drop in income of £35 and with a slight increase in expenditure, we closed the year with a deficit of £75 2s 8.

A similar drop in income is noticeable in the Bowling and Putting Green and Tennis Sections.

It is satisfactory, however, that after five years of war our investments remain untouched.

DISTRICT WELFARE FUND.—There is no income for this Fund during wartime, and the balance remains unaltered at £2/1/1.

MEMBERSHIP.—During the year 6 men, 9 ladies, and 9 youths resigned from the Club, while 7 men, 1 lady, and 14 youths were admitted. The membership now stands at 111 men, 65 ladies, and 49 youths, and of this number 66 men and 4 ladies are serving with H.M. Forces.

We offer our congratulations to Fl/Lt. J. R. C. Affeck, D.S.O., D.F.C., A.F.M., R.A.F.V.R., on his adding to distinctions already gained, and to Fl/Sg. Donald Fraser, R.A.F., on his distinction in gaining the D.F.M.

The Secretary will be pleased to learn of any other member of the Club who has been similarly honoured.

PRIZE WINNERS FOR 1944.—Hillside Trophy—Mr Charles Spiers ; Victory Cup—Surgeon-Commander C. E. Brittain and Mr Charles Spiers ; Grand Fleet Cup—Mr James Findlay ; Cameron Cup—Mr James Findlay ; Challenge Cup—Mr J. A. Burnett ; Youth's Trophy—John Turnbull ; Thomson Trophy—Alan Sutcliffe.

ABERDOUR GOLF CLUB.

ABSTRACT OF ACCOUNTS for the Year to 30th November, 1944.

1. GOLF COURSE.

INCOME.

1943.							
£13 10 0	ENTRANCE FEES :—						
	8 Gentlemen	...	£12 0 0				
	1 Lady	...	1 1 0			£13 10 0	
201 10 0	ANNUAL SUBSCRIPTIONS :—						
	75 Gentlemen	...	£112 10 0				
	61 Ladies	...	60 10 0				
	49 Youths	...	21 5 0		194 5 0		
	VISITORS' TICKETS :—						£273 13 6
	1676 Daily at 1/-	...	£83 16 0				
	21 Daily at 2/-	...	2 2 0				
	7 Weekly	...	2 12 6				
	3 Fortnightly	...	1 10 0				
	6 Monthly	...	4 10 0				
	2 Youths	...	0 12 6				
	149 Friends	...	3 14 6				
	25 Service	...	29 15 0		128 12 6		
175 1 6	LOCKER RENTS (Members)	...			9 5 0		
9 12 6	GOLF BALLS, TEES	...					
1 0 0	INTEREST :—						
	Halifax Building						
	Society	...	£5 0 9				
	Tennis Loan	...	14 8 0				
	War Loan	...	3 13 8				
23 0 9	Bank	...	0 0 7		23 3 0		
— —	DEFICIT	...	...		75 2 8		
£423 14 9					£443 18 2		

EXPENDITURE.

1943.					
£290 9 1	UPKEEP OF COURSE, CLUB-HOUSE, &c.—				
	Wages and State Insurance	...	£247 8 6		
	General Repairs	...	9 2 8		
	Upkeep and Upkeep	...	10 5 9		
	Repairs to Machinery	...	23 17 6		
	Motor Spirit, &c.	...			
	RENTS, TAXES AND INSURANCE :—				
	Rents—				
	From Military Authorities, Compensating Rent—	£96 14 0			
	Clubhouse	...	£20 0 0		
	Course 23 15 0		44 5 0		
126 8 4	Taxes	...	£52 9 0		
	Insurance	...	17 17 9		127 3 10
	MANAGEMENT—				
	Honoraria, Printing and Stationery	...	£10 10 0		
	Postages and Miscellaneous	...	11 12 8		
		...	3 17 7		£26 0 3
13 1 3	Less—Proportion charged to Bowling and Putting Greens and Tennis Courts	...	6 6 0	19 14 3	
1 15 0	SUBSCRIPTIONS	...		1 1 0	
4 0 0	PRIZES (Youth's Club)	...		10 0 0	
5 0 4	DEPRECIATION	...		4 0 0	
	SURPLUS	...			
£423 14 9				£443 18 2	

16

THE YEARS 1949-1970

The end of the war and the subsequent restoration of the Course signalled the start of a new phase in the development of the game of golf at Aberdour. Several milestones would be reached and passed during this 20 year period which would transform and shape the future of the Club. Despite the war and the subsequent upheaval to the course, Aberdour was still one of the most popular and attractive venues for Golf in the East of Scotland and maintained a high level of visiting clubs. Visitors were considered essential if membership fees were to be kept at a reasonable level as well as providing the funds to keep the course in first class condition. Many of the changes were designed and implemented with a view to improving facilities for both members and visitors and to securing the future of the club.

Bill Cochrane recollects:

"In 1952 and 53, I spent my summer holidays working on the course as a "Student Green Keeper" along with others including a companion (and well known fellow in the village at the time), Rab Simpson, nicknamed Sambo by his friends, the younger son of the then Professional, Dave Simpson. We were told by the Head Greenkeeper, Mr Thomson, to dig up a pipe which was sticking out of the ground in a rose garden in front of the Clubhouse.

We duly dug down and down, probably four or five feet, but the pipe continued straight down. Eventually we started to uncover a large concrete plaque on which was depicted the Polish National Emblem. As you know, the course was used as a camp for the Polish Army during the war and in our unsuccessful endeavours to take the pipe out we had stumbled upon their emblem which, one has to assume, they had placed outside the door of their HQ, which later became (and was beforehand) our wooden Clubhouse located just inside the main entrance on the left hand side."

The first milestone to be passed was in 1949 when for the first time golf over Aberdour was allowed on Sundays. This was quite a major step forward because Sunday golf was not all that common in Scotland. Earlier attempts to introduce golf on the Sabbath had failed primarily because Moray Estates were reluctant to give their consent, but also because many members were still opposed to the idea. However, attitudes to recreation and sport on Sunday were gradually changing and the motion obtained the required majority at the 1949 AGM. As a result members were allowed to play for the princely sum of one shilling per game, in addition to the annual subscription.

Perhaps it was just coincidence, or was it that there were more opportunities to practise at weekends, but in 1950 Aberdour Golf Club,

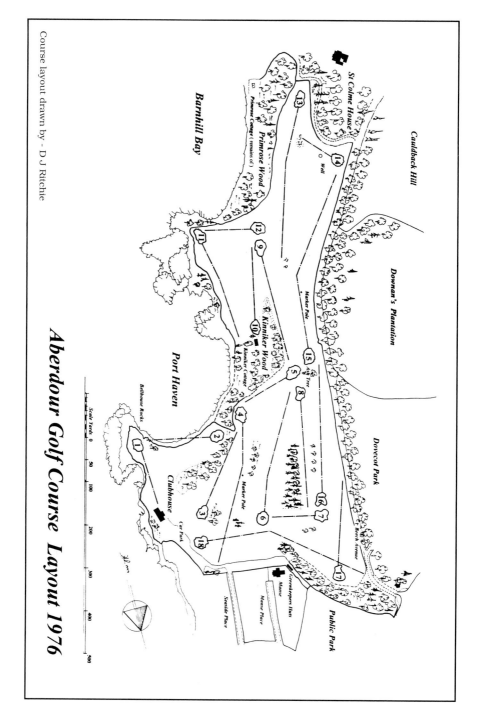

Aberdour Golf Course Layout 1976

Course layout drawn by - D J Ritchie

Cauldback Hill

St Colme House

Barnhill Bay

Primrose Cottage (remains of)

Primrose Wood

Wall

Downan's Plantation

Kinniker Wood

Kinniker Cottage

Marker Pole

Tall Tree

Dovecot Park

Port Haven

Bellhouse Rocks

Clubhouse

Car Park

Marker Pole

Beech Avenue

Greenkeepers Huts

Manse

Manse Place

Seaside Place

Public Park

Scale Yards 0   50   100   200   300   400   500

for the first time, won the Fifeshire Advertiser Cup team championship. The team on that occasion was Walter Ogg, Donald MacKenzie, Eric Kirkham and Jimmy Findlay. It also signalled the start of an era for the Club's outstanding player of the fifties and early sixties, Walter Ogg. He was to go on and win the Club Championship no less than ten times and achieved success in Fife County Championships and many open scratch competitions in Fife. In 1961 he set a course record of 58 over the 4424 yards par 64 course. He was honoured by the Club for his golfing achievements by being given life membership in 1965.

At this stage it is worth recording an event held in the summer of 1952. An exhibition match was held over the Aberdour Course on a Monday evening in July which attracted a crowd of over 500 spectators. This fourball match, held in aid of the King George's Fund for Sailors, consisted of four very prominent Scottish golfers of that era including one of our own Aberdour members, Eric McRuvie, an ex-Irish Open Amateur Champion and member of the Walker Cup team. Eric's partner for the evening was Jean Donald from Gullane, Scottish Ladies' Champion and a member of the Curtis Cup team and they were up against formidable opposition in the persons of Moira Paterson, Lenzie Ladies' Champion and member of the Curtis Cup team and Jack McLean, Gleneagles, ex Scottish Amateur Champion and member of the 1932 and 1934 Walker Cup teams. The game produced some very fine golf with Paterson and McLean the eventual winners by 4 and 3. Both returned scores of 65. The event was such a success it is surprising that this type of event has never been repeated at Aberdour.

The second significant milestone of change was reached in 1957. I am sure many of our present day members cannot imagine a golf club without a "nineteenth" - well, that was the situation at Aberdour until that year. It must be said that the lack of a bar had neither affected membership levels or the popularity of the course with visitors. Times were changing and the provision of better facilities for both members and visitors was considered necessary not forgetting the attraction of additional revenue from a licensed bar. Consequently, after several failed attempts to gain the required majority at an AGM, the motion to apply for a licence was carried and eventually granted by the local authority. The kitchen at the far end of the old cottage style Clubhouse was converted for use as a bar and Mrs Wood became the Club's first stewardess. Perhaps small and cosy might be an apt description of the lounge/bar area, certainly a far cry from our present day facilities. Although it was another step forward, the need for more modern premises was becoming more apparent every day. More and more people were playing golf and Aberdour's popularity was such that over 11,000 visitors tickets were sold in 1961.

At that time a major drawback to embarking on expenditure of a large scale was the existing arrangement with the Moray Estate Development Company whereby the ground on which the Clubhouse and Course lay was leased on a year to year basis. This hurdle was finally cleared in

1961 when the Council were able to negotiate a 20 year lease of the course at an annual rent of £250. In addition they were able to feu 4000 square yards of ground from the entrance to the course to the end of the car park. The timing of this new arrangement was particularly important as new houses were being built overlooking the course in Dovecot Park. The cost of a new house in Dovecot at that time started at £2,830. Having achieved a much more permanent arrangement over the lease of the course, the question of improved Clubhouse facilities could then be faced. The choice was either altering the existing building which had served the Club for almost 60 years or a complete new Clubhouse. A sub-committee was set up to explore the various alternatives and to submit proposals and plans for discussion and approval by members at a general meeting. This meeting was held in November 1963 and approval given for the construction of a new Clubhouse at a cost in the region of £16,000 on a new site at the end of the existing car park and immediately behind the 16th (Bellhouse) (now the 1st), thus taking advantage of the panoramic views over the Firth of Forth.

John Reid, an architect and Club member, was responsible for producing plans for the new Clubhouse and he also agreed to act as adviser to the Club during construction. As adequate funds were available, thanks to an excellent response from members to the Council's appeal for loans, work was to start almost immediately with a view to completion for the commencement of the 1965 season. This was achieved with the official opening ceremony, by Miss Helen M Somerville, the Club's oldest Lady member, taking place on Saturday 25 May 1965.

The photograph shows Miss Somerville with the Council at the entrance of the new Clubhouse on opening day.

Bill Allan recalls:

'During the appeal for loans to finance the building of the new Clubhouse, I was approached in the car park by a member who announced, 'I hear you're looking for money for the new Clubhouse' and, with the Secretary looking on, he proceeded to count out several hundred pounds on the boot lid of his car, saying - 'Now, I don't want a receipt, I don't want any interest and I only want the money back if I need it - but I don't think I'll need it - and I don't want anyone to know about it.'

Some weeks later, the Secretary received a letter from a lady member, complaining of a group of gentlemen golfers playing without their shirts - this group included the generous benefactor. The Captain and Secretary were in some dilemma but in the end the wisdom of Solomon prevailed and the Captain replied, pointing out that it was an extremely hot day and that such conditions were unlikely to be repeated for five or ten years but whenever similar conditions did prevail, the same privilege would be extended to the lady members!

Members can see from the photograph below that a number of constructional changes have taken place since then. Changes have also been made internally. How many members remember the bar being where the trophy cabinet is today and the folding partition between the lounge and dining area? The view from the lounge window has changed too with the construction of the terminal at Braefoot Bay. Small motor boats conveying sightseers to and from the "Black Sands" (West Beach) to Inchcolm have

been replaced by tankers, the occasional one drifting to within a good wedge shot from the first tee! Nevertheless, despite the increase in merchant shipping traffic, seals still swim in the bay and bask on the rocks below the Clubhouse window.

This busy and momentous 1965 season in the Club's history closed with the retiral of Johnny Bald from the Council. Match Secretary for many years, also a past-Captain and Club champion, he had the unique distinction of serving on the Council since 1922. For his service to the Club he was made a life member.

Progress during the sixties was not simply confined to the Clubhouse and facilities. There were many significant alterations and improvements to the course. In 1961 water was provided for all greens and the following year the six foot high mound topped with a large concrete slab in the middle of the first fairway (the present 17th) was finally demolished and the ground levelled. This mound was a relic from the war situated roughly where a good drive landed. A direct hit on the concrete slab added considerable yardage to one's drive and there were many tales of long driving records.

1967 saw the first change to the course layout for many years. With the new Clubhouse now well established it was felt that the first tee was situated too far from the Clubhouse and Professional's shop. As a result the then 16th (Bellhouse), 17th (Firs) and 18th (Roundal) holes were changed to become 1st, 2nd, and 3rd.

The following year additional land to the south of St Colme House was obtained from the Moray Estate Development Company (MEDC) for the purpose of course extension. This was followed in 1969 by an offer from MEDC for the Club to purchase the existing course plus additional ground being considered for a course extension (including Kinniker Wood and Cottage) at a price not exceeding £12,000. This offer was considered and approved by a Special General Meeting in November 1970.

This period in the Club history ended with the destruction of two of the oldest landmarks on the course. This first to go in 1970 was the famous Ash Tree which stood beside the green of the longest hole on the course. It acted as a very useful guide for the approach to the green and also as a useful marker for the tee shot to the former short 5th (Wicket) hole. The long par 5 was named after it and although it is now our 10th hole, over the years it will be remembered by many as the 8th, 12th or 15th. Severely damaged by gales the old ash tree had to be removed and replaced by a semi-mature tree. Now after 25 years, the replacement tree although still not as tall as the original tree, has grown sufficiently to provide a useful marker. The base of the original tree can still be seen to this day. The other landmark to pass into history was Kinniker Cottage. The name may be unfamiliar to many members but it and its occupants were an integral part of the course until age caught up with it in 1970. It was situated behind the green of the par 3, 200 yards, 7th hole, later the 10th, and the hole was named after the cottage. It had various occupants over the years, perhaps the most well remembered being Andrew Smith and later George Todd. Many a drive overshot the green and rolled under the hedge into the garden which was only a few yards away and, of course, was out-of-bounds. By 1970 the cottage was unoccupied and was boarded up in 1971. It was finally demolished in 1977 and today there is little sign of the once picturesque cottage. The present 4th green was constructed in the cottage garden.

Finally, the Captains and members of the Council during this 20 year period are to be congratulated on bringing the many changes to successful and satisfactory conclusions. Many of these stalwarts have passed away but some such as Bill Armit, Bill Allan, David Colman, Andrew Wotherspoon and Harry Connell are still going strong. Sadly, Bob Walker, Secretary for 15 years to February 1971 and Club Captain in 1978/1979, the man on whose shoulders the bulk of the work fell and who played a major part in negotiations with Moray Estates, died during Centenary Year.

THE YEARS 1971 - 1995 _____

When the gates at Seaside Place were first opened for golf at the turn of the century, few would have imagined that one day a round of golf at Aberdour would take them as far as Monks Cave at Charleshill. Situated at the extreme point of the headland facing Inchcolm Island, the cave was reputed to be used as a shelter by monks while waiting for the boat to cross to the monastery on the island.

Now with the acquisition of the additional ground at Charleshill, the Western Boundary of the course was soon to be extended to within a stone's throw of the cave. Not since 1914 when the course was extended from nine to eighteen holes had such a major course alteration been planned. Initially the project suffered set-backs and delays. Planning permission was refused due in the main to objections by the tenant farmer who was reluctant to give up use of the fields but in 1977 a second application was successful.

A golf course architect, Mr Fraser Middleton, had been commissioned to draw up plans for three new holes in the Charleshill fields and members were also asked by the Council to submit ideas and plans for a new course layout. The response from members was excellent. Sixteen proposals were received and after due consideration Harry Clegg's submission was declared the most suitable. In addition to the construction of three new holes, many alterations were made to the existing course. New tees were built at the 3rd (Ainsley's Pier), 4th (Cottage) and 11th (Manse) holes, a new green constructed at the 4th, a new path built from the 2nd (Firs) green along the water's edge to the 3rd (Ainsley's Pier) tee. A new path was made to the 10th (Ash Tree) tee which was re-built and a new tee and green at the extended 5th (Oxcar) - the former Heich Green being adapted. As a result of the changes three of the existing short holes, Wicket, Heich and Cauldback, were lost forever although the Cauldback Green and surrounding ground was retained as a practice area. It was to be 1983 before the Charleshill extension was ready for play and 1985 before the revised 18 holes layout was completed. A new SSS of 67 was confirmed in 1986 and the course has remained more or less the same since then.

As if the foregoing changes to the course were not enough, around the same time nature also took a hand in altering the scenery. Dutch Elm disease was discovered among many of the trees surrounding the course, initially in Kinniker Wood but eventually spreading to other parts of the course. The woods bordering the 6th (St Colme) and 16th (Avenue) holes were particularly hard hit. Almost the entire Primrose Wood at the 6th was affected by the disease and it became necessary to fell and burn some 60 to 80 trees. The sea suddenly became visible from this fairway, probably for the first time since the course opened. What had been a well sheltered part of the course was now open to the sea breezes.

A programme of tree planting was started under the supervision of Bill McRae and some 100 new trees were planted throughout the course.

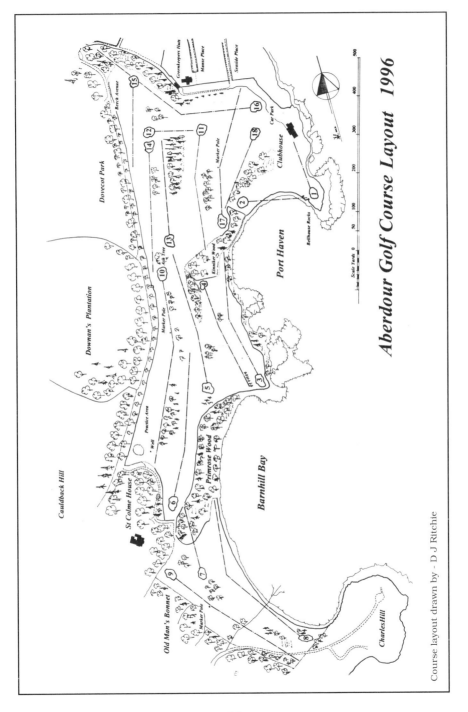

Aberdour Golf Course Layout 1996

Course layout drawn by - D J Ritchie

25

The young trees are now well established, although it will be many years before the woods, which were a feature of Aberdour, return to something like their former state.

Although some members and even some of the regular visitors to Aberdour were critical of the longer course and the long walks from green to tee, the course extension did go some way to easing the congestion on the course.

More and more people were playing golf and for the second time in the history of the Club waiting lists for all categories of membership were introduced in 1972, a situation which has continued to the present day.

The influx of new members led to a greater percentage of male members participating in competitions and morning, afternoon and evening starting times were introduced on medal days. As our records show, the number of trophies for annual competition accelerated rapidly during the seventies and eighties. Another innovation was the introduction of monthly medals on Wednesday. The increase in competitions was not just confined to the summer season. For many years the only winter competition was the "New Year's Day Bottle" but 1971 saw the start of the Winter Foursomes which to this day has a faithful following. Monthly medals were also introduced during the five winter months and inter-club winter leagues became a permanent fixture.

With the increase in the number of competitions and more competitors it was not long before new course records were set. In 1976 David Ritchie shot a 56, six strokes under the SSS of 62, the lowest score recorded on the short course. Two years later as a result of a slight change to the course, new tee at the 11th (Ainsley's Pier) hole, a new record of 57 was set by Lance Sloan. In 1984 on the newly extended course, but with the short Cauldback hole still in play, Stuart Meiklejohn set a new target of 61 (SSS 67). Finally in 1990 Stuart set the present record of 63 on the 5469 yard layout.

The tournament increase was not just restricted to members only competitions as Aberdour was soon to join other Scottish Clubs in introducing Open Amateur events. The first Aberdour Open for men was held in September 1973 with the Mixed Open following in 1974. There was no doubting the popularity of these events as entries were soon over-subscribed and as a result Opens were soon to be introduced for ladies, seniors and juniors. Another extremely popular event which has attracted large entries over the years has been the Invitation Greensomes which has been running since 1979.

The resultant increased workload for the Match Secretary together with a general increase in administration led eventually to the need for modern office aids to ease the workload and a computer was purchased in 1988. After initial teething troubles the benefits of the purchase were soon evident. Of course not everyone in the Club was computer orientated and when members were first asked to enter their own scores on the computer there was many a laugh as people struggled to master the intricacies of the keyboard. Now, years later, it has become a routine operation thus allowing the Match Secretary to produce detailed print-outs of scores very quickly and also provide members with a variety of hole-by-hole statistics.

Possibly Aberdour's finest and most consistent golfer, Stuart Meiklejohn, came to the fore in the early 70's and to this day has retained his form, remaining one of Fife's leading golfers.

In the early 1970s lengthy periods of severe drought conditions caused major headaches for John Robb, the Head Greenkeeper, and his staff. 1973 in particular was a very bad year and the situation was exacerbated by the authorities imposing restrictions on the use of water. As a result, the mains water supply which provided the, then fairly limited, course watering system, was suddenly cut off.

For several months the greenkeeping staff made heroic efforts to keep the greens and tees from completely drying out. This included the transportation of a large tank of water on the back of the tractor to the worst hit areas. By far the worst was the exposed 18th green which over the summer gradually turned a lovely shade of brown.

In an effort to overcome this serious situation and, if possible, to prevent it happening in the future, the Council took the unusual step of arranging for a water diviner to go over the course with his divining rod to establish if a supply of water was readily available within the course boundaries. Out of the four sites identified by the diviner as suitable for the sinking of a borehole, the Council selected the one adjoining the 16th (Avenue) tee and close to the perimeter of the course. A six-inch borehole, costing approximately £600, was considered adequate for the job.

It was to be early 1974 before drilling was underway but the outcome was successful. An adequate supply of water was discovered at 180 feet. Later that year, the engineers, at a further cost of £700, installed the pump, control system and additional pipes to enable the new equipment to be connected to the existing watering system.

Despite the success of this project, it became obvious over the next 20 years that sooner or later, because of normal wear and tear, the club would have to invest in a more up-to-date watering system. The solution arrived in 1994 when an unexpected windfall came the way of all golf clubs.

It was announced that VAT on annual subscriptions had been wrongly imposed since 1990. All the clubs could expect to be reimbursed the full amount plus interest. In Aberdour's case the refund would amount to £66,000 plus interest. As the money was to be used for the benefit of all members, it was decided at the 1994 AGM to install a new computerised watering system to replace the old system which was inadequate and labour intensive. The new system, costing £60,000, included new piping and pop-up sprinklers on greens, tees and some fairways. The installation was completed by June 1995.

The Clubhouse underwent three major changes during this 25 year period. In 1974 a Clubmaster's house was added to the Eastern end of the existing Clubhouse and some internal alterations were made to the lounge. The main change was the moving of the bar from the wall where the trophy cabinet now stands to its present position. The second major alteration took place in 1989 when the Clubhouse was extended to include a members' lounge, cellar, office, juniors' room, and a professional's shop. The third and final development came as a result of concern among members as to the poor condition of the existing facilities in the gents' locker rooms. As a result a Special General Meeting was called in November 1993 to discuss and vote on proposals to extend and upgrade the locker rooms and to refurbish and upgrade the main lounge in time for the Centenary Celebrations. The total cost of the proposals was £135,000. The motion was carried and the work on the locker rooms was completed by May 1994. It became necessary to call a second Special Meeting on 13 February 1995 to approve additional costs in connection with the refurbishment of the lounge. The revised proposals were approved with the work finally being completed by June 1995.

Trophy winners 1986

CENTENARY YEAR 1996 _____

THE BUILD UP

Once it was agreed that Aberdour Golf Club's Centenary Year would date from the constitution of the Club in 1896 and not 1905 when the Club moved to its present location, it was decided to form a Centenary Committee to plan the celebrations to mark the first 100 years of the Club's existence.

In June 1991, the Council invited Bob Pearston, a past Captain of the Club, to undertake this task. As teamwork rather than protocol was considered to be essential to the project, he was left to create his own Committee. Bob realised he needed a Committee who were experienced in administration and essentially enthusiastic to work together over a period in excess of five years culminating in the Centenary Year in 1996. With this in mind he gathered around him a team of experience and initiative and ended up with an interesting blend of talent.

An important objective of the Centenary Committee was to provide advance funding for a comprehensive programme of golfing events and social functions to run throughout Centenary Year but the most challenging aspect of the remit given to the Committee was that the fundraising should not detract from the level of revenue normally attracted to the Club.

Considerable time and effort went into the many enterprises and functions held over the years preceding Centenary Year. These included the recruitment of sponsorship, the setting up of the 200 Club, plant sales and coffee mornings, numerous social evenings and a grand prize draw. A range of Centenary mementoes was also available to the membership of the Club which included limited editions of prints illustrating various aspects of the Course, bottles of whisky and wine, ties, scarves and crystal.

With sponsorship complementing the various fundraising activities and strong support coming from members and friends, the Committee raised sufficient funds to subsidise the Club's Centenary celebrations without making any demand on the Club's financial resources.

Immediately preceding Centenary Year a colourful souvenir Centenary brochure was provided to every member of Aberdour Golf Club detailing the comprehensive programme of golfing events and social functions which would take place in Centenary Year. The brochure included special articles by Peter Alliss and Arthur Montford, profiles of outstanding club players, poems, a centenary quiz and numerous photographic aspects of the course. The souvenir brochure was also freely available to the large number of visitors who played over the course in Centenary Year.

CENTENARY FIXTURE LIST

Compiling a programme of golfing events for Centenary Year was a fair challenge, especially at the time of the first meetings in 1991. 1996 seemed a long way off and it was very difficult to anticipate what would happen and would really be expected from the golfing fixtures during Centenary Year. It was also extremely difficult to envisage how certain previously untried events would turn out. However, as things got underway in 1991, one of the first targets was to arrange a meeting with a Club whose members had only fairly recently celebrated their own Centenary Year. Contact was made with Glencorse Golf Club and meetings were arranged with George McGregor, ex Walker Cup Captain, and their current Centenary Captain and Committee to discuss the way their Centenary Celebrations were handled.

Rough budget expectations were used as a basis for the targets set at Aberdour especially with regard to the financing of the golfing fixtures. The size of the programme in relation to other Centenary events and cognisance taken of the normal annual club events had to be carefully looked at. The way in which sponsorship was obtained was also discussed at length, this obviously had a major bearing on the types of event that could be held at Aberdour. It was necessary to charge a small entry fee for some of the special Centenary events. This was kept as low as possible and was based on the overall budget strategy.

The main objective of the Centenary Fixture List was to obtain the correct balance of fixtures to encompass as many members as possible and because of the already full club fixture list, many events had to be scheduled outwith the normal competition days.

The Centenary Committee also considered that it would be an honour to host some of the major County events during Centenary Year. Arrangements were made with the Fife Golfing Associations to host the Gents', Ladies' and Seniors' County Championship during 1996 and also the prestigious Scottish Ladies' Foursomes.

THE CENTENARY YEAR

The Centenary celebrations were suitably launched at a Civic Reception and Dinner held in the City Chambers on Friday 19th January 1996, hosted by Dunfermline District Council. A representative group of 70 members attended the function at which a trophy, "The Seniors Centenary Cup", was presented to the Club by Provost Margaret Millar JP who commented favourably on the Club's contribution to tourism in Fife. On behalf of the Club, the Ladies' Captain, Miss Jean Bald, presented Provost Millar with a framed limited edition print of the 1st (Bellhouse) hole.

The reception was followed a week later with over 140 members and friends attending the Burns Supper in the Queensferry Lodge Hotel. The same venue was used for the Ladies' Dinner in February followed by the Gentlemen's Dinner in March. All were outstanding successes with Carole Michelle (Mickey) Walker, Captain of the Solheim Cup Team, principal speaker at the Ladies' Dinner and the large turnout at the Gentlemen's Dinner was entertained by a trio of excellent speakers in the persons of John Stark, Senior Professional at Crieff GC, Sandy Jones, Executive Director of the PGA and Jim Watt, ex World Boxing Champion.

The Fife Ladies' Golfing Association was invited to hold the Fife County Ladies' Championship at Aberdour in Centenary year on Sunday 14th April 1996. In damp and windy conditions, Elaine Moffat of St Regulus Golf Club became Fife County Champion for the first time with a one hole victory over Fiona Lockhart of Balbirnie Park Golf Club. The other semi finalists were Dorothy Ford of Scotscraig Golf Club and Susan Johnston from Burntisland Golf Club. The Patrick Trophy and the Junior Cup were won by Louise Kenney of Pitreavie Golf Club. Mrs Helen Thomson, a past Ladies' Captain of Aberdour, won the Coronation Medal with a net score of 70.

Sunday 21st April saw the first scheduled Centenary event for Club members - a Texas Scramble. What a start! - the first Centenary event of the year and it had to be postponed due to fog. By 0930 hrs you could not even see beyond the 1st tee, let alone the 1st green. To play under such conditions would be extremely dangerous and the Committee were left with no alternative but to postpone the event until later in the year.

The first major Centenary event took the form of a Professional - Amateur competition. This was a previously untried format even by Scottish PGA standards but during pre tournament meetings there was an eager enthusiasm for this completely new format proposed by Aberdour Golf Club, whereby the top 12 Order of Merit Scottish Professionals were invited to Aberdour to play with teams of 6 Aberdour players who each played 9 holes.

Prior to the event, in fact 2 or 3 days beforehand, the Scottish PGA tournament caravan was located at the 1st tee in readiness for the Sunday's event. This set the scene and raised the expectancy levels accordingly. On the Sunday, everything was ready for what was to be a memorable day for all who took part. After checking in, 72 Aberdour members met their respective Professionals at the designated practice range for the day, an area adjacent to the side of the 16th fairway. The SPGA kindly let us borrow over 2,500 of their tournament golf balls to be used during the practice session. The Professionals then gave a one hour golf coaching clinic to their team members, each member having his / her own personal coaching session during the period, following which the teams then retired to the Clubhouse at around 12.20 hours to take some lunch prior to the shotgun start.

While the players were in the Clubhouse, there was the small matter of collecting up the 2,500 golf balls from all areas of the 16th, 17th, 11th and 18th fairways - and some other areas wider afield - in around about 30 minutes!! When looking along the 17th fairway, such was the quantity of golf balls in a confined area, it actually appeared as if an isolated snowshower had occurred on the fairway. However, a team of juniors was assembled and, with the aid of a van, a few large buckets, a great deal of effort, and a few sore backs, the areas of the course were cleared on time to allow play to start promptly.

A novel feature of this event was that out of the team of 6 Aberdour players, only 3 played at any one time. The other 3 players then gave their support until it was their time to play at which point their clubs had to be ferried out to the changeover tees at the appropriate time. The clubs of the finishing players were then brought back to the Clubhouse. The logistics and co-ordination were carried out by Bob Pearston and Jack Gray without a hitch.

Upon completion of play, all players enjoyed a superb buffet in the Clubhouse. The winning team, with an aggregate score of net 120 (b.i.h.) comprised Susan Farrar, Colin Gray, Gavin Hughes, Gary Polland, Jim Thomson, and Iain Watt playing with their professional David Thomson of Kings Links Golf Club. The winning professional was Colin Gillies of Falkirk Golf Club who returned a scratch score of 66.

Next event on the Centenary calendar was Centenary Gamblers - a most unusual format and certainly unique to Aberdour. In this competition 18 teams of four tried to accurately predict how they would score around Aberdour Golf Course. The odds offered were related to a team's predicted score, the three best net scores counting in relation to par and a net three under par at a given hole would receive better odds than a team predicting level par at the same hole. A team failing to meet its prediction would lose its fictitious (£60) stake at that hole.

At the end of the day, it was not necessarily the best team that won, but rather the team that more accurately predicted what it could achieve. As a result, it opened up the possibility of winning to the majority of teams in the field.

All those who played thoroughly enjoyed the day and each match had its own degree of pressure as teams tried to achieve their targets. Perhaps sometime in the future this kind of competition could be included in the annual fixture list.

The competition was won by the team of Iain Watt, Bill Cross, Ian McDonald and Club Captain Willie Crowe with an imaginary financial return of £4,890 from 18 x £60 bets. In second place, with a return of £4,500 was the team of Andrew Hubble, Ian Dickson, Norman Henderson and Graham Milne, while the team comprising veterans Bob Pearston, Noel Marsh, Hugh Hanlon and Bill Hutchison rather over-estimated their golfing abilities and finished 'bankrupt'!

The June celebrations got off to a very successful start with 100 Aberdour players taking part in a mixed foursomes match with Murrayfield Golf Club, also celebrating their Centenary in 1996. Arrangements for this match started with meetings between the two clubs in 1993 and representatives of both clubs met every 6 months to progress the organisation of this event. Budgets, format of the match, handicap limits, catering, were all high on the agenda. As we approached Centenary Year, meetings were more frequent and it became fairly apparent that the logistics involved in ensuring that players from both clubs arrived timeously without having to wait for too long prior to their match, were fairly complex. A quick bit of computer programming sorted this out. A shuttle bus service was operated between both clubs.

The first matches started at 0900 with the last tee off being 1500 hrs. A running buffet was operated at both Clubs and in the evening suitably engraved crystal wine jugs were exchanged as a memento of the occasion.

Aberdour triumphed overall winning 19 - 6 at Aberdour with our away team narrowly beaten 14.5 - 10.5. Overall match result Aberdour 29.5 Murrayfield 20.5. A great day was had by all those taking part.

CENTENARY WEEK

Without doubt the highlight of Centenary Year were the celebrations held from 16th to the 22nd June. The weather could not have been more kind with warm sunny conditions during the week. This was an added bonus as many of the social functions were accommodated in a large marquee which had been erected on the putting green adjacent to the Clubhouse.

Sunday
The week got underway on the Sunday Morning with a mixed foursomes competition over 12 holes with the competitors dressed in 1896 period costume. The foursomes was won by Sandy Laing and Lois Hutchison with a net score of 45, with Lenny Wahlroos and Betty Mackay the runners-up

Period Dress Competition

John Train, Jean Bald, Jessie Pearston, Bunty Smith, Mike Dowling, Chris Twaddle and Merilyn Laing

Interring the Time Capsule in Commemorative Cairn
Mark Laing and Ben Durkin

Ladies Centenary Dinner

Babs Crichton cuts Centenary Cake - Mickey Walker, Greta Armit, Babs, Jean Bald, Provost Margaret Miller J.P.
Lady Past Captains and Honoured Guests behind

Gents Centenary Dinner

Burns Supper Friday - John Khin gives The Immortal Memory Address
Jean Bald, Elizabeth Khin, Rev. John Scott, Willie Crowe, John Khin and Karyn Crowe

Pro-Am Competition
Stan Robb gets some coaching

Pro-Am Competition
The Winners - D. Thomson, C. Gray, G. Polland, S. Farrar, J. Thomson, G. Hughes, (missing I. Watt)

Competitions for Centenary Cups

Bob Pearston, Maggie Christie, Karyn Crowe, Graham McEwan, Jessie Pearston, Willie McKay, Willie Crowe.

Front - Ewan Crozier and David McNeil

Centenary Ball
A happy group arriving for the Ball

with a score of 45.7. Prizes in the period dress competition were awarded to John Train, Flora Dickson, Bob Halliday, Lois Hutchison and Patricia Ritchie. This event was followed immediately by a short ceremony to mark the raising of a specially designed Club Centenary flag donated by the Ladies' Section and the interring of a sealed time capsule containing Club memorabilia, in a commemorative cairn close to the 18th green. Bill Armit, the longest surviving past Captain of the Club had the honour of raising the new flag. The whole ceremony was watched by a large gathering of members and friends including every surviving past Captain of Aberdour Golf Club, and the proceedings were recorded on camera by Club photographer George Taylor, perched precariously on the roof of the clubhouse. A highly successful opening day ended on a high note with wine, a buffet meal and music and dancing in the marquee.

Monday

The ladies' interclub competition was held on Monday June 17th. 12 local clubs accepted invitations to compete along with 6 Aberdour teams. With the best 3 net scores out of 4 counting, the winning visiting team was Kirkcaldy with a score of 220. The winning Aberdour team of Irene Stuart, Margaret Steele, Marjorie Crawford and Sheila Robb returned a score of 214. A complimentary buffet was available throughout the day for competitors.

Tuesday

The Aberdour Seniors' Open was held during Centenary Week and Match Secretary Jimmy Johnston reported the competition over-subscribed by early April. Always a popular event, competitors came from all over Scotland and the north of England. On this occasion, local knowledge proved a great advantage and the first two places were taken by Aberdour veterans:

| Winner - | Tom Ward | 79 - 16 - 63. |
| Runner-Up - | Eddie Geraghty | 87 - 23 - 64. |

Wednesday

It was the turn of the Seniors to take centre stage. Members aged 65 and over competed in a pairs Stableford Competition for the Seniors' Centenary Cup which had been presented to the Club by Dunfermline District Council. The competition, with a shotgun start, was held over 12 holes starting at the old 1st (Kinniker) and to add to the occasion the Wicket and Cauldback holes were reinstated for this event.

At a buffet prize-giving ceremony in the marquee, the winning team of Archie Kerr and Rita Chorley, with a score of 30 points, was presented with the Centenary Cup by the former Lady Provost Margaret Millar. Bob Halliday and Stan Wilson came second with 27 points. Following the prizegiving, the company was entertained with a programme of songs by the Wemyss Maxwell Group.

Thursday

The gentlemen's interclub team event took place on the Thursday when ten invited local clubs took part with the team from Pitreavie Golf Club picking up the winners' prize with a score of 205. Six teams from Aberdour Golf Club took part and the winning score of 197 was posted by David Ritchie, Mike Dowling, Willie Crowe and Lenny Wahlroos. A complimentary buffet was available throughout the day for competitors.

Friday

A special competition for Sponsors was held on the Friday with a representative group from the club comprising Council members, past Captains and past Club Champions acting as hosts. Following a welcoming refreshment and light buffet lunch, the teams presented themselves at an allocated tee for a shotgun start.

Sixteen teams took part with the winners being Castleblair - Gordon Forbes and Frank Pajak and Aberdour's Hugh Hanlon - producing some brilliant golf to record a scratch score of 59.

A convivial evening following this event when a substantial buffet meal and wine was served in the Clubhouse.

Saturday

June 22 was Centenary Day and again the sun shone.

Because of the large entry for the competition for the Centenary Trophies and having regard to the planned evening festivities, it was necessary to bring forward the starting time for the competition to 0630 hours and at that early hour three bleary-eyed golfers, Bill Hay, John Train and Bill Twaddle made their way to the 1st tee. Close on 140 members took part and, at the end of the day, the respective winners and runners-up were:

Centenary Trophy for Gentlemen

Winner	Willie McKay	76 - (16) - 60
Runner-Up	Ian Maxwell	80 - (18) - 62

Centenary Trophy for Ladies

Winner	Maggie Christie	90 - (22) - 68	
Runner-up	Elizabeth Rae	89 - (19) - 70	(bih)

Centenary Trophy for Juniors (played over 12 holes)

Joint Winner	Euan Crozier	56 - (15) - 41
Joint Winner	David McNeil	57 - (16) - 41

In the evening a reception was held in the marquee which was followed by a substantial meal and complimentary wine. The presentation of the Centenary Trophies took place after the meal when the winners received their trophies and prizes from Mr Graham McEwan of Shell Expro who, together with Exxon Chemical, had donated the lovely Claret Jugs. Other leading competitors received their prizes from Mrs Karyn Crowe, wife of the Club's Centenary Captain.

The happy gathering concluded the evening by dancing into the "sma' 'oors" to the music of 'Jack Gray and Friends'.

Without doubt, the Centenary Week was one of the most enjoyable and memorable in the long annals of Aberdour Golf Club.

Although the main Centenary celebrations fell in the month of June, a number of popular and successful golfing and social events were held in the second half of the year.

Two team competitions were held in August. Firstly, a Tri Am competition for teams of three players - any combination of gents and ladies - with prizes being awarded for the lowest net score with the team's best ball, the lowest net score with the second best ball and the same for the third ball. The McGlynn family team of Audrey, Mike and Alistair were successful returning a lowest best ball score of 52 - the highlight of the round being a net zero by Audrey at the 15th hole.

It was the turn of the Heggie family, Walter, Willie and Greta, ably supported by Paul Smith, to triumph in the second team competition, taking the form of a Texas Scramble.

The last major golf event was the Celebrity Am tournament held in September. This event had been organised in conjunction with the Charity, Stars Organisation for Spastics Scotland, and many well known stars and personalities from TV, stage and the sporting world turned out despite a rather wet day. 35 teams of 4 players took part in the competition, each team comprising either a celebrity, sponsor, sponsor's guest and an Aberdour member, or 3 Aberdour members plus a celebrity. Past Captain Noel Marsh and his wife Sheena had kindly donated a trophy for the winning team - Alec Hutt, Sandy Laing, Scott Christie and Lindsay Hamilton from East Fife FC. The longest drive competition was won by Gordon Durie, Glasgow Rangers FC, with a drive of 309 yards at the 11th. Full marks to Gordon, a member of Scotland's International Football team, who arrived home from Vienna less than 24 hours earlier after playing in a World Cup qualifying match against Austria.

Many fundraising events took place throughout the day. Ally Logan, one of the celebrities, created a great deal of interest and excitement when asked to auction three autographed footballs kindly donated by Dunfermline Athletic, Heart of Midlothian and Glasgow Rangers Football Clubs. A very professional and highly entertaining auction raised a further £255 for the charity.

At the end of the evening a cheque for £3,500 was presented to 'Stars Organisation for Spastics, Scotland'. Neville Taylor, on behalf of the Charity, expressed his thanks to all those involved in what was a truly magnificent effort, the first time that the club had ever staged such an event.

A substantial buffet was available throughout the day for competitors, donated by the Woodside Hotel (Aberdour Golf Club Catering Limited).

The Centenary Ball, held in November in the Dunfermline Conference Centre, brought the Centenary Year Celebrations to a very successful conclusion.

Winter had just set in and the approach roads to the Conference Centre were covered with frozen snow and ice, making driving somewhat hazardous. The members and guests attending the function were extremely relieved when bus transport was provided to and from the Conference Centre.

The Club Captain, Centenary Chairman and their wives had just taken up position to receive and welcome the arriving guests when the fire alarm sounded and everyone, arriving guests and Conference Centre staff, were ushered out of the buildings into the chill evening wind, to await the arrival of the Fire Brigade. Fortunately this did not take long and the firefighters arrived in about four minutes. After a quick and thorough examination of the Conference Centre, the incident was proved to be a false alarm and the welcome and reception of guests was allowed to proceed.

About 120 members plus a number of special guests, which included the President of the Scottish Golf Union, Dr George Gormley and the President of the Scottish Ladies' Golfing Association, Miss Joan Lawrence, were present at this formal function.

An excellent five course meal preceded the Ball when excellent music for dancing was provided by the band 'The Late Shift'. During the evening a competition was held with the proceeds being donated to the Charity 'Children in Need'.

An excellent evening of fun and fellowship passed all too quickly for all who attended.

At the end of the evening's entertainment, Bob Pearston, Chairman of the Centenary Committee, was presented with a certificate of Life Membership in recognition of his input to the highly successful programme of golfing and social events held during Centenary Year.

THE WAY AHEAD

A Perspective on the Future
1996-2096

The memorable Centenary Year, so rightly celebrated, is now history and happily we can reflect on so many pleasant and lasting memories of a wonderful period in the history of Aberdour Golf Club.

However, anniversaries are always occasions for looking forward as well as back. Therefore, with the new millennium almost upon us, perhaps it is advisable to give thought as to how we might speculate on the years ahead. Do we just sit back complacently and merely be grateful for what we have inherited? The answer should be an emphatic "NO". Hopefully the ambitious membership will have the vision to formulate a constructive future policy well into the next century. In consequence here are a few notions, albeit not for immediate action but for the record, as to some possible objectives as and when the appropriate time can be defined.

Let us assume firstly that, if predictions are accurate, the lifespan of the Braefoot terminal runs out say in about 30 years' time, acreage could thus become available for future development of playing facilities in that general area (enough ground for another Course - the new West Course). Furthermore St Colme House, no longer required by the present owners, would serve excellently as the location for our next Clubhouse.

Without doubt, positively an interesting objective. With careful planning there would be room available (a) on the course, and (b) in the Clubrooms leading to facilities available to a much greater number of golfers having more leisure time, early retirements will all lead to an increase in demand to participate in the game of golf. Increased numbers would subsidise the funding,especially if the Club could be further developed beyond that of a traditional Golf Club i.e. amenities so as to become the centre of an entire family's social life. Space precludes a detailed range of such suggestions but the perception could be as follows :-

New West Course : Land acquired for a possible Championship course at Braefoot - all floodlit. Fantastic range of possibilities in a superb location, - the finest in the Country !

East Course : the present course to be reinstated to the pre-1980 format. Again outstanding views, unbelievable layout renowned as one of the best in all Scotland and restoring the popular layout for the majority of members and visitors ("Tomb-Stone Summit and Death Row Trail" eliminated). Starting points would be centrally controlled from the new clubhouse.

The New Clubhouse would accommodate not only meeting rooms, family size dining room, fitness centre, gents' and ladies' locker rooms, party rooms , a "Seventh Heaven Lounge" (19th) but also a world of indoor golf simulation inclusive of weather control and video / computer analysis of the swing. This would be the control centre for all activities, the golf shop, a two tier driving range (heated) ; large Astroturf putting green complete with contour simulators; and an expansive fairway complete with 3 target greens. All floodlight and weather protected to permit play throughout the year. Soon technology will provide opportunities for even wind and breeze, cloud and sun before we know it. This is only a glimpse of a subject of endless fascination with much yet to come. All this within stretching distance of the main building.

Funding of the aforementioned prognosis even through the next century will be considerable but there will be a fantastic change in lifestyle as a result of the anticipated world wide technological revolution into the millennium. Some judicious forward planning could well see the foregoing facilities in place to be enjoyed by future members in the club's Bi- Centenary Celebrations.

Up to now, we have looked at the future prospects of Aberdour Golf Club from a fairly realistic and, arguably, conservative point of view. But what if we take this a stage further, let our imagination run riot for a while, and consider these possibilities.....

The Present Clubhouse and Car Park : What will happen to this area should we eventually move to St. Colme House?   Would the existing clubhouse be modified to provide a Five Star sporting lodge or hotel complex, offering accommodation, catering and sporting facilities specifically for golfers but with the option of a bit of fishing, sailing etc. Developed properly, this would have the potential to provide the Golf Club with a substantial income from what is undoubtedly a prime site.

The Helicopter Shuttle Park established at the previous Braefoot Terminal would be brought into service for the convenience of visitors and VIP's arriving from afar to enjoy a golfing experience at "Royal Aberdour". A monorail might also be considered linking the Helipad, Clubhouse and Sporting Lodge.

A round of golf :- from a playing point of view, things could really start to get out of control.

As new technology more and more takes over all our lives, think for a moment as to what it might do to a round of golf. It may well be that we are all armed with computer key-pads which will record all information regarding strokes played and relay these back to the clubhouse as they happen. The strokes would automatically be logged onto a centralised computer system which would generate leader boards, control handicaps, etc. The key - pads would also give the player an analysis on how the shot was played, what went wrong and suggest the necessary corrections for the next shot.

The Rules of Golf would be readily available from the computer key-pad and in a moment's search the appropriate rule would be displayed and the options available to the player.

Counselling would be available after every major competition in the Seventh Heaven Lounge (and for some players even before playing off).

Golf Equipment : If new technology allows us to record correct scores etc, will golf equipment be also controlled electronically. Will we all set off from the first tee with one computer controlled club? This all purpose club could be programmed, through your key-pad, of course , to the correct loft and weight required to hit the shot. This would certainly make it physically more relaxing playing around Aberdour having only to carry one computer controlled club and your key -pad. You would also have your golf ball, yes, ball in the singular, as it would come complete with micro chip making it impossible to lose!! A left handed "twitch "glove guaranteed as a cure for bad putters and the yips might well be approved by the R & A.

Weather Conditions :- as we all know, the wind can play havoc with our game, especially on some of the exposed places at Aberdour. How many times have we heard the late starters bemoan the fact that they had the worst of the conditions or vice versa. Will we all eventually play under the same climatic controlled conditions? Yes ! you've guessed it, by the central-ised computer system in the Clubhouse. Certainly this would be fairer to all concerned, wouldn't it?

When the founding fathers of Aberdour Golf Club met in 1896, what visionary dreams did they hold for the development of the Club and the game of golf. Did they foresee the 'guttie' being replaced by the 'Balata' ball? Or the hickory driver giving way to a titanium head/carbon shafted driver, or golf clubs being transported round the course on a power operated trolley or golf buggy? At the end of the nineteenth century such developments would have been considered a pipedream and somewhat far-fetched.

As we stand at the threshold of a new millennium, the latter comments of this section of the book may now appear humorous and also far-fetched, but in this accelerating age of electronic technology development who would be brave enough to discount the possibilities that lie ahead?

With **'virtual reality'** now used to control robot buggies millions of miles from Pasadena, is it not conceivable that one day golfers may arrive at the course with their electronic partner that they would send out on the course whilst the member would sit back in the Seventh Heaven Lounge, controlling his partner's moves while sipping quietly a cool glass of beer and watching the seals gambolling on the rocks below.

Never! Never! This development is extremely unlikely, as the game of golf will always remain a challenge of golfers against all the elements of nature. This would certainly rule out **'virtual reality'** with electronic part-ners!

But wait a moment! Could this resource become 'the alternative game

Row Trail', playing their round of golf in the comfort of the Seventh Heaven Lounge and maintaining their love and interest in this game of golf. Well, only time will tell!

In consequence perhaps we should ask ourselves at this stage- **"why do we become involved in this stupid game?"**

The answer to such a question is well summed up in a quote many years ago, by the great Bobby Jones, which read something like:-

"This is a fickle, infuriating, cruel, unforgiving pastime but I would not live my life without it. Despite it being an egocentric game, it has provided for me, and I am sure for you, a lifetime of friendships and camaraderie surpassed by no other".

The future is bright - let's go for it.

THE SENIORS

At Aberdour the initial step which recognised the need for a Competition restricted to senior members of the Club was taken by Miss Somerville as far back as 1965 when she presented the Club with the Veterans' Trophy. This was, and still is, a match play competition for gentlemen members over age 60. The following year a Trophy for a Senior Ladies' competition was presented by Mrs J McLeish.

From then until 1980 there was virtually no expansion of senior golf at Aberdour. However, by this time early retirement was becoming more and more common and the next 10 years was to see a fairly rapid expansion in senior golf not only at Aberdour but throughout Scotland.

A Senior Invitation event was added to the fixture list in 1980 followed by the Charles Hawkins Trophy in 1982, the latter being awarded to the best placed Aberdour player in the Invitation competition. The increase in competitions together with a full fixture list of friendly home and away team matches with neighbouring clubs in Fife was sufficient to justify the introduction of a Senior Convener post to organise and generally oversee senior golf within the Club.

Don McQueen was a popular member of the Club for many years and when he passed away in 1989 his wife presented the Club with a trophy for Senior competition. The decision to make it a 3 club plus putter competition gave it an unique place in our list of Club competitions.

Finally in 1990 Aberdour joined the ever-growing list of clubs running an annual Gents' Seniors' Open event and following on from this, a few years later a Senior Ladies' Open Competition was introduced at Aberdour. In recent years these open events have proved extremely popular. Early entry is essential as most are over-subscribed. Many of our members compete regularly in these Open events and numerous successes have been recorded over the years.

All-in-all senior golf is flourishing and is now firmly established in the golfing calendar.

THE LADIES' SECTION

Ladies have been associated with the Club since its formation in 1896. At the outset there were only 16 ladies playing golf but, like all sections of the Club, as popularity for the game of golf increased, so did membership of the ladies' section. Mrs J Oliver was first elected Ladies' Captain in 1906 and by 1912 lady members out-numbered the men 94 to 83.

Apart from the war years, the number of ladies continued to climb resulting in compensating increases to the maximum membership allowed under the rules. This figure now stands at 160 and a waiting list is in operation.

Although ladies do not enjoy full membership they have complete freedom in running their own AGM and electing office bearers. In fact records exist of ladies' Annual Meetings from as early as 1906 although it was to be 1929 before the ladies' section was finally constituted. This was followed by attaining membership of the Ladies' Golf Union in 1936.

Entries for ladies' competitions were extremely low in the early years. The first ladies' trophy was the Club Cup, competed for in 1898 on the course at Couston, followed by the Hewitt Medal and Yearly Cup in 1906 on the new course at Seaside Place. As membership increased so did the number of competitions and trophies and now ladies compete for ten major Club trophies annually and other one day events such as the Flag and Novelty Competitions. In keeping with the men they have a fairly extensive fixture list including friendly matches with Burntisland, Canmore, Milnathort, Dunfermline, Dunnikier, Pitreavie, Balbirnie and Kirkcaldy. Details of the main Club competitions with winners are given in Appendix 4. In 1980 a Ladies' Open was added to their calendar with the winner receiving the Royal Bank Trophy. This trophy was presented to the Club by the Aberdour Branch of The Royal Bank of Scotland. Mixed Foursomes competitions have always proved very popular at Aberdour Golf Club and in the mid 1970s a Mixed Open Competition was introduced. From 1984 the competition was contested for the Robert Pearston Cup.

> **Robert Colman recalls** *"I will soon be approaching 50 years of membership at Aberdour and have many happy memories as a Committee member and also on the Course. One story that always sticks in my mind was an instance where I was playing in a mixed foursome event at Aberdour a few years back. The pairings arrived at the 1st tee and one of our lady members rushed up to her partner and introduced herself " I'm Mary and I am 36".*
>
> *Her partner, one of the Club's noted characters, quickly replied "Is that your age, handicap or bust size ?"*

It is somewhat surprising that an official Ladies' Club Championship was not introduced until 1960. The records show that initially the junior

Championship was dominated by two players, first Joan Lawrence and then by Jean Bald, both having won the title of Lady Club Champion no less than 12 times in the period 1960 to 1987, a quite outstanding achievement.

Over the years Joan and Jean have brought many honours to Aberdour Golf Club and no history of the Club would be complete without highlighting some of their many achievements. Both are well known in Ladies' National and County golfing circles on both the playing side and the administration side. Joan was outstanding in the sixties, winning the Scottish Championship three years in a row, 1962-64 and also a Scottish internationalist 1959-1970, then crowning her golf career as an international selector and chairwoman of the LGU in 1989. Jean, while not achieving the dizzy heights reached by Joan, still has a formidable list of achievements for a local Aberdour girl. A Fife and East of Scotland Champion on several occasions over the period 1965 to 1982, a Scottish Internationalist 1968, 1969, 1971, Scottish Team Captain in the 1985 European Team Championship and finally an International Selector 1988-1991.

However, time marches on and the last ten years or so have seen a change in the Club honours board with new names coming to the fore. Yvonne Sloan first captured the ladies' title in 1981 and now has five victories to her credit while Rosemary Scott has also won five times since 1989, Rosemary's fifth victory coming in Centenary Year when she defeated Yvonne by 2 and 1 in the final. Both have also performed well on the County scene.

Finally one veteran lady member is worthy of a mention. Babs Crichton has been a member since 1950 and in her heyday captured the East of Scotland Ladies' Championship and later the Scottish Veterans' at Gleneagles in 1977. Still competing at the age of 80, may she continue to enjoy her golf at Aberdour for many more years to come.

It is perhaps not surprising that the current ladies' course record was set by one of the above mentioned players, Jean Bald, when she recorded a 66 in August 1984 against a SSS 67. This record was set with the short Cauldback hole still in play.

THE JUNIORS

Membership of the Club was open to young people from day one. Initially interest was low, there being only 3 junior members when the Club was formed in 1896. This state of affairs remained well into the nineteen twenties. In fact the first mention of a competition for youths at Aberdour was in 1932 by which time junior membership had increased dramatically to 48. No trophy existed for the period 1932 to 1936 but in 1937 the Captain Mr J G Jack, presented the young people with their first Club trophy, the Youths' Trophy. Initially competitions were held over 10 holes with each game having a senior member as a marker, a format which was maintained until 1982 when it was decided to hold competitions over the full 18 hole course.

During the Second World War youth interest remained at a high level and many good young players emerged during this period. The need for more competitions was apparent and 1945 saw the introduction of a second competition, the Whitehouse Trophy. This trophy was donated by Mrs Whitehouse and family in memory of her late husband. Commander Holly Whitehouse RN, who lost his life in the sinking of HMS Barham by enemy action on 25 November 1941.

Young girls too were now becoming more interested in the game of golf and as a result, the Whitehouse Trophy in 1956 and the Youths' Trophy in 1957 were won by the same girl, Miss Charlotte Finnie.

By 1960 the junior section was well and truly established. Strong support was forthcoming from parents, club members with a keen interest in the development of junior golf and a succession of Club professionals who helped enormously by giving lessons during school holidays. As a result standards improved and for the next 20 years or so Aberdour juniors compiled a long list of success in Fife County Championships.

Graham Milne won the Fife Boys' Championship in 1962 then crowned his junior career by winning the British Boys' Championship at Gullane in 1965. 1962 also saw the start of our best juniors being allowed to compete in the Men's competitions. This undoubtedly helped in their development and in 1972 Stuart Meiklejohn achieved the honour of being the youngest winner of the Men's Championship at the tender age of 15. As the list of achievements in Appendix 6 shows, the impetus started by Graham was carried on by a succession of very fine golfers, many of whom progressed into the senior ranks and are still members today.

A Junior, having accepted the invitation to compete in a Senior Competition, was no longer eligible to play in the Junior Section.

During these successful years and even the next decade, one man stands head and shoulders above the rest in the promotion of junior golf at Aberdour. Bob Taylor devoted much of his spare time to organising the competitions, arranging of markers and generally promoting and encouraging junior golf. In recognition of his work at junior level he was awarded the Torch Trust Trophy in 1977 and subsequently Life Membership of Aberdour Golf Club, fitting rewards for his many years of hard work.

The first Boys' Open was introduced at Aberdour in 1988 and was a great success and some years later a Girls' Open was inaugurated. One only needs to compare the early days with the situation today to appreciate fully the gigantic strides junior golf has taken particularly in the last 50 years. Popularity, of course, has brought some drawbacks. Some of our current senior members started golf at a very early age. Now we have a minimum age restriction of 11. Membership limit now stands at 80 - a far cry from the early years - and in addition there exists a waiting list in the region of 60.

ABERDOUR GOLFERS

Information on the achievements of Aberdour golfers in the early years is extremely sparse, although a course record of 80 was set by Willie Binnie on the Couston Course in 1897.

The re-location of the Course at Bellhouse Park, the subsequent transition from a nine hole to an eighteen hole course and the outbreak of hostilities in 1914 no doubt all contributed to the lack of information on the golfing scene. It must also be recognised that competitive club golf in this period was still very much limited.

Interest in the game of golf returned slowly after the end of the First World War and there is little evidence of the achievements of the golfers from Aberdour within the Club records. Jim and Johnny Bald, Bob Cuthill and Donald MacKenzie were all recognised as golfers of considerable repute whilst Ian Moyes (who could outdrive most contemporaries using a No. 1 iron) established a course record of 63 in 1935.

In the late 1940s, after the restoration of the Golf Course to eighteen holes, and into the 1950s, Walter Ogg had the distinction of carrying the Aberdour banner throughout the Kingdom of Fife and beyond with considerable success.

Enthusiasm for the game of golf then gathered pace and Joan Lawrence was an early standard bearer for Aberdour Golf Club, winning the Scottish Ladies' championship three times and becoming a member of the Curtis Cup Team. Joan's successes were soon followed by Graham Milne when he broke through a very talented field of golfing potential to achieve a major success by winning the British Boys' Championship at Gullane. These successes raised the profile of Aberdour Golf Club and also the enthusiasm of the younger membership of the club and other major successes were soon registered by Jean Bald, Stuart Meiklejohn and several other members, whose profiles are given later.

In 1971, the Fife Golfing Association introduced the Fife Boys' Team Championship, The Lightbody Trophy, with the inaugurating event being played over Kinghorn Golf Club. Aberdour's team won the event and thereafter retained the trophy for four consecutive years.

PROFILES OF ABERDOUR GOLFERS _____

JOAN LAWRENCE

Joan Lawrence is certainly one of Aberdour's most successful golfers, her career is littered with success at the highest of levels. Joan has been competing now for more than 50 years, 38 of which she has been a member of Aberdour Golf Club, during which time she won the Ladies' Championship on 12 occasions.

On the national scene, Joan was a member of the 1964 Curtis Cup Team, helped Scotland to second place in the World Team Championship the same year and was a member of the winning Vagliano Cup team in 1963 and 1965. She was Scottish Ladies' Champion for three years in a row from 1962 and continued the high standards by winning the Scottish Veteran Ladies' Championship, again three times in a row, the first of these successes coming in 1982. Joan was a regular member of the Scottish Team for some 12 years. A regular Fife County player for 30 years, Joan won the Fife Ladies' Championship 18 times, the first of these successes coming in 1953.

Joan's support for golf at all levels is well noted. Not only has she been involved competitively at the highest level but has also been involved in the administrative and organisational aspects of Ladies' golf and has had many honours bestowed on her. In 1989 Joan became Chairperson of the Ladies' Golf Union and in 1995, she was President of the Scottish Ladies' Golfing Association. She was also President of the Scottish Veteran Ladies' Golfing Association from 1994 to 1995. Joan was the winning Captain of the Great Britain and Commonwealth Team in 1971 and Vice Captain of the Curtis Cup Team in 1970 and has been involved in selection committees at all levels.

Joan feels that her overall successes in golf are down to accuracy off the tee combined with a fairly strong short game. Her overall game has held good for a very long time and is well adapted to the variety of courses she has played over the years.

Joan was a member of Aberdour Golf Club's Centenary Committee and her experience and advice were invaluable in the lead up to Centenary Year.

GRAHAM MILNE

Graham has been a member of Aberdour for some 33 years. As with most Aberdour golfers, his game is based on a strong short game and an ability to putt fairly well on Aberdour's tricky greens.

The major success of Graham's golfing career was in 1965 when he won the British Boys' Championship.

Graham had the distinction of never once taking three putts on any green during the entire Championship - a skill obviously developed from playing his golf at Aberdour.

Whilst competing as a junior, Graham won the junior section of the 1963 Fife Boys' Championship, the first competition he had ever entered, and in 1965 won the Scottish Midland Counties Boys' Championship. Graham was a regular member of the Fife County Boys' Team and also played regularly for the Fife Men's Team at district level. He won the Fife Men's Championship in 1970 with two excellent scores of 69 at Scotscraig. During the 70's, Graham won various local amateur competitions around Fife and has been Club Champion at Aberdour on eight occasions.

Graham has served on the Committee at Aberdour as Greens Convener and subsequently Club Captain from 1989 to 1991. He was a member of the Centenary Committee with responsibility for competition fixtures during 1996.

STUART MEIKLEJOHN

Without doubt, Stuart Meiklejohn must rate as one of Aberdour's finest golfers. Still at a fairly young age, Stuart has achieved so much in such a short time. His allegiance to Aberdour Golf Club is without question and he can always be relied upon to support both club and team events no matter the conditions or time of the year.

One of Fife's leading golfers for some years now, Stuart has been a regular member of the County Team since 1973 and to date, his performance in local amateur competitions shows more than 20 wins to his credit in 36 hole events, with a similar number of 18 hole wins. He was the youngest winner of the Aberdour Club Championship and has been Champion of the

Club for more than a decade.

Stuart considers that consistency from the tee to green has contributed to his success over the years. He considers that his putting could be better but judging from his performance, it certainly can't be too bad!

Stuart has been both Fife Stroke Play and Match Play Champion, has won the Fife Champion of Champions event on three occasions, led the Fife Order of Merit in 1988, 1992, 1993, 1994, 1995 and 1996 and perhaps his most prestigious win to date was in the East of Scotland championship at Lundin Links in 1993. Stuart also won the Fife Champion of Champions in 1996. The standard of amateur golf is fairly high and this is illustrated in the 1994 Leven Gold Medal where Stuart shot 16 under par for the four rounds, only to finish second.

During the late 70's, Stuart spent some time playing on the Scottish Professional circuit. He qualified for the British Open in 1980 and 1981, won three assistants' tournaments in 1977, finished 16th in the Scottish Order of Merit in 1979 and in the top 150 in the European Order of Merit in 1980 and 1981.

JEAN BALD

Jean Bald has been a member of Aberdour Golf Club for over 40 years now and one of its best lady golfers. Jean has a good all round game which has served her well over the years but it is probably her short game that would be considered as her strongest asset.

On the national scene, Jean was victorious in the East of Scotland Ladies' Championship in 1965, 1973 and finally in 1982. She reached the semi final of the Scottish Ladies' Championship three times and represented her Country both in the Home Internationals and in the European Championships. She was a member of the winning Scottish Team in the Home International matches in 1969. Jean has also been the winner of

the prestigious Babe Zaharias Trophy.

In partnership with Yvonne Sloan, she was successful in winning the Scottish Ladies' Foursomes Championship in 1975 and again in 1982.

At County level, she was Fife Champion seven times during the period 1966 to 1982 and has represented the County for around 30 years.

Jean is very committed to the support and promotion of ladies' golf. She has captained the Scottish Girls', Junior Ladies' and Ladies' Teams for the European Championships and has also been involved in many Committees over the years. Jean has undertaken the duties as an LGU International Selector, and is at present the LGU Representative on the Scottish Ladies' Golfing Association and has been President and Captain of the Fife County LGA along with her Captaincy of Aberdour Ladies.

DAVID DIBLE

David Dible has been a member at Aberdour for some 30 years and, in fact, started his playing career at Aberdour. In his earlier days, David regularly partnered Stuart Meiklejohn in foursomes matches and the two were very formidable opponents and always extremely difficult to beat.

A stylish swing combined with a solid golfing technique meant that David was always going to be destined for good things and, in 1971, he won his first event, the Fife County Boys' under 14 Championship.

Further success was to follow in 1973 when David, by now playing some of his best golf of his career gained an international cap when selected for the English boys' Team. David gained his place in the team following a 36 hole trial at Rosemount, Blairgowrie. After a solid first round of 74 David was well placed to make the team. However, things looked less promising when in the second round he was six over par after four holes. Fortunately David held his nerve and played the remaining 14 holes in five under par to record a 73 and comfortably make the side that beat Scotland in the international match that year. In the week that followed David enjoyed a strong run in the British Boys' Championship eventually losing in the semi-finals to David Robertson, the eventual winner.

At County level, David played for both the Fife Boys' and Fife Men's County Teams. In fact, in the five years which he represented the County, he never lost a singles match - a remarkable achievement.

David's best score at Aberdour is 60 but what makes this more amazing is that it was his first ever senior medal at Aberdour - some introduction! Away from Aberdour, David once scored 59 round Glencorse in a University Match against the home club, the round also including a hole in one.

As with all Aberdour members, David's game is built on a very strong short game although he feels that his putting sometimes could be better.

NEIL HILL

Neil, who has played golf at Aberdour for most of his golfing career, has built his game on a high level of consistency from tee to green. As a result, he can always be relied on to turn in a good score whether playing as an individual or as a team player. With a best score of 65 around Aberdour and an eclectic competition best of 52, Neil has proved his ability to master the tricky Aberdour course.

In his earlier years, Neil won the Fife Boys'/Youths' Stroke-play Championship in 1980 and then, some 16 years later, in Centenary Year, was a beaten finalist in the Men's Match-play Championship. In 1982, Neil was a member of the Scottish Universities Team. During his successful period in the early 80's, Neil was a regular Fife Boys' Team player.

The most memorable occasion of his career was a University trip around all the top golf courses in Ireland including Ballybunion, Lahinch, Royal Dublin, Portrush, Newcastle County Down. We can only assume that it was memorable for the golf and not, allegedly, for the jars of the famous dark liquid that may have been consumed on the odd occasion !

DEREK MILLER

Derek has been a fine player for many years now and, during Centenary Year, continued his good form when victorious in the British Ministry of Defence Championship held at Dalmahoy. Playing for the MOD, also in 1996, Derek was part of the successful team that won the Civil Service Team Championship.

The previous year, 1995, saw Derek crowned Scottish Civil Service Golf Champion.

It is not only recently that Derek has proved his ability on the golf course. In 1979, he was a regular player in the Fife Boys' Team, a team that went on to lift the prestigious Gary Harvey award when winning the Inter County Team Event. In 1986, in quite stormy conditions, Derek won the Aberdour Open Trophy with a fine score of 69, the only player in a strong field to break 70.

At Aberdour, Derek has a fine score of 64 to his credit which came in the last round of the Club Championship in 1985. His game is built round some very strong iron play, especially the low irons although he feels himself that short shots around the green could be improved upon.

It is not only on the golf course that Derek's interests lie. He is involved with his own Golf Section at work and has been an active member of Daniel Stewart's and Melville College Golf Club for some 10 years now.

BEN ELDRED

The name of Ben Eldred is synonymous with Aberdour - ask any local about Ben Eldred and he will be instantly associated with our Club. This is understandable, when you consider that Ben has played all his golf at Aberdour - some 44 years, in fact. If you needed someone to be relied upon

around Aberdour, whether it be in a stroke play or match play format, then Ben would be your man. Ben's controlled game is ideally suited for Aberdour, he is credited with no less than 6 holes in one to his name, and whilst his handicap is now 9, for a long time Ben played as a category one golfer with a handicap of 2.

The undoubted highlight of Ben's career, and one which gave him the most satisfaction, was his well deserved success in the 1962 Club Championship.

Ben relishes the challenge of a good game and understandably enjoys the foursomes format of team and inter club matches. He has been a member of many winning teams, the highlight perhaps in winning the Nairn Trophy on four occasions. He also represented Aberdour in the final of the Daily Express Pro Am final at Haggs Castle few years back with the team finishing a very creditable 7th.

Ben has also served on the Council at Aberdour and has worked on both the Greens and House Committees.

ANDREW HUBBLE

University golf arguably belonged to Andrew from 1977 to 1983. In 1977, he won the British Universities' Stroke Play Championship and was runner-up in the same event in 1980. The most remarkable achievement came during 1980 to 1983 when he was the first Scottish University Graduate to win the Scottish University Golfing Society Championship four years running. He was also a member of the winning team in the British and Scottish University Championships in 1979 and 1980 respectively.

Almost unnoticed during all this was the small matter of winning the R & A Gold Medal (The St Andrews Links Championship) in 1980 - a fine achievement in such a prestigious event.

Further success followed in 1981 when Andrew was the top golfer in Fife, in leading the Order of Merit and winning the Mackay Bowl. Andrew's good form continued and in 1984 he won the Lothians Champion of Champions event.

A frequent County player at all levels between 1972 and 1987, Andrew helped Fife to many successes over the years.

Andrew considers his most memorable achievement was in winning his first Club Championship in 1976 with an average score of 62.5 for each of the 4 rounds - not many would argue with that. As far as weaknesses are concerned, Andrew considers that he was at his most vulnerable after lunch during some of the University matches - no doubt he was talking about a liquid lunch !!

Andrew has served on the Council at Aberdour for 6 years and was Greens Convener in 1990 and 1991.

DAVID RITCHIE

Between 1974 and 1976 David was very prominent in Junior Golf in Fife. This purple patch in David's career contributed to three successive team victories in the County Boys' Championships and brought individual successes in the Boys' Stroke-play championship in 1975 and the Match-play Championship in 1976. David had further success in many other junior events including the Elie and Dunnikier Boys' Opens in 1975.

These fine achievements were ultimately rewarded when David was selected for the Scottish Schoolboys' Team in 1975. David also represented Fife at all levels including the full Men's Team in 1976.

David is yet another Aberdour golfer whose success has been built on a strong short game - combined with a fair degree of accuracy off the tee. These factors enabled David to record a magnificent score of 56, 7 under par, during a Club Medal in 1976. Full details of this spectacular round are to be found elsewhere in the book.

Whilst having such a good spell during the mid 70's, all David's successes did not come easy. One in particular, the 1975 Dunnikier Boys' Open, found four boys tied on the same score. After the better inward 9 rule was implemented, only one boy was eliminated. The last 6 and last 3 holes failed to eliminated any further boys and it was by virtue of David's fine birdie at the last that enabled him to take the title on a countback.

YVONNE SLOAN

Yvonne has always been one of Aberdour's best lady golfers.

She learned her golf caddying for her father and competing with the boys in the Junior Section under the convenership of Bob Taylor who ran a very disciplined Junior Section. In her early years as a junior it was apparent she had the talent to become a successful golfer.

During the period 1970-1974 Yvonne won many Girls' Open Competitions along with Junior County Championships from 1972-1974, gaining her a regular place in East of Scotland Girls' Teams over this period.

On a national level, in 1974 she reached the later stages of the British

Girls' championship, beating on the way the then World Junior Champion and in the semi-final of the Scottish Girls' Championship, losing to Dale Reid. Yvonne was selected for the Scottish Girls' Teams of 1973 and 1974.

The transition from Junior to Senior Golf took no time at all and in 1975, along with Jean Bald, won the Scottish Ladies' Foursomes, a success which they repeated in 1982.

Yvonne has been a regular competitor in the Fife County Ladies' Championship, being runner up on three occasions, and has been a member of the County Team from 1974 to 1995. During this period Fife qualified for the Scottish County Finals on four occasions culminating in victory at Prestonfield Golf Club in 1995.

Her golf has been built round a fine long game, by her own admission - *'I hit the ball like Tarzan but chip and putt like Jane.'*

With a best score of 63 (six more than her brother Lance's Course Record of 57) round the the original Aberdour Course and a 68 round the present layout, combined with a lowest handicap of 2, her overall game cannot be that bad!

Within the Club Yvonne has served on the Committee for two periods and was Ladies' Captain from 1983-1985. She has also served on the Fife County Ladies' Golfing Association Committee from 1983-1988 and was elected Captain from 1986-1988.

She is currently Fife County Ladies' Golfing Assocation Junior Convener, putting back into golf time and effort in response to the pleasure the game has given her.

WALTER OGG

For the period after the war right through until the early 70s, Walter Ogg was undoubtedly Aberdour's finest golfer. Wattie, as he was always known, knew every blade of grass, every bump, every borrow around Aberdour and this, combined with an extremely well grooved swing, meant that he was always going to be such a difficult player to beat.

It was not only at Aberdour that Wattie's golfing skills came to the fore. In 1949 he won the Leven Gold Medal and later that year, the Dunfermline Cup. During the 50s, he won the Battle of Britain Golf Competition and reach the semi-final of both the Eden Tournament and the Highland Open - no mean achievements considering the high quality of players taking part in these events. In 1960, Wattie won the Fife Matchplay Championship, played at St Andrews.

At Aberdour, Wattie was nigh unbeatable in scratch competitions and he was Club Champion 10 times, his first success coming in 1949. You would be hard pressed to find any trophy at Aberdour for which he was eligible to compete that did not have his name on as a winner at some point in time during his career.

Wattie was a strong supporter of Aberdour and, where possible, always turned out for representative matches and team competitions and led the club to many successes throughout the years.

Wattie passed away in 1997 and will be sadly missed.

PRESS CUTTINGS

MALCOLM TAYLOR
Extract from the DUNFERMLINE PRESS - July 1988

"LOCAL HERO - Prize guy...that's Malcolm Taylor with the magnificent Fife Youth's Matchplay Trophy"

"ABERDOUR'S Malcolm Taylor was the toast of the local golfing fraternity this week after pulling off arguably the biggest shock of the County season to win the Fife Youths' Matchplay Championship.

Despite the event being held over his home course, Taylor was expected to have little chance in a line up which included the likes of Scottish Boys' Champion Colin Fraser and Alan Mathers, holder of the Youths' and Senior Fife Strokeplay titles.

Malcolm with caddie Mark Laing

But the 16 year old from Dalgety Bay showed little respect for reputations, and beat both Fraser and Mathers on his way to lifting the title at the first attempt.

It was a remarkable success considering that while Mathers and Fraser play off plus one and one respectively, Taylor has a handicap of six.

And Aberdour's local hero was first to admit that his triumph was a surprise. "What with knowing the course, I believed I had a chance, but not a great one" he told the Press. "It is undoubtedly the best win of my life, and I hope it will earn me recognition at County level".

Taylor qualified for the event by finishing joint fifth in the Stroke-play Championship the previous week, but was expected to be heading for an early exit when he was drawn against Scottish Internationalist Mathers in the first round.

However, he left his opponent in a daze after winning the first three holes, and, after increasing that lead to 5 up at the turn, the result was never in doubt. Mathers won two holes to cut the deficit to three, but a half on the 16th hole was enough to give Taylor a 3/2 win.

That set up a semi final against Ballingry's Stephen Payne, and while the pair were evenly matched most of the way round, Taylor edged in front at the crucial stage to win by two holes.

The final was an even closer affair, with Taylor leading by a hole at the turn before Fraser, from Burntisland, forged ahead at the 13th. But after doing so well to reach the final, Taylor wasn't going to give up without a fight, and, after squaring the match at the 15th, he clinched a victory he is unlikely to forget for the rest of his life when he rolled in a 12 foot putt for a birdie two at the last.

ANGUS McNAUGHTON

Dundee Courier and Advertiser - May 1974

"McNAUGHTON IS FIFE MATCH-PLAY CHAMPION"

This was the headline that met Angus McNaughton's fine success in the 1974 Fife Match-play Championship at Balwearie. The report continued:-

"A magnificent drive to within 18inch of the flag at the 279 yard seventeenth hole at Balwearie, Kirkcaldy, yesterday, clinched the Fife Match-play Championship for Angus McNaughton. This gave him a 2/1 win over Murray Mitchell, St Andrews, who will have cause to remember a few missed putts.

McNaughton got away to a flying start by winning the first three holes. The Mitchell putter had one of its few bright moments at the long 5th pulling one back with a birdie from six yards.

McNaughton restored his lead with a birdie 3 at the 8th but conceded the 11th after twice being out of bounds. The Aberdour man moved three ahead again with a 5 at the long 12th.

The St Andrews man made a late burst winning the 15th and 16th to reduce the deficit to one. But he missed his putt for a three at the 17th and conceded the 18inch putt."

On his way to the final, Angus had notable wins over two of Fife's leading players at the time, Tony McIntyre and Tommy Cochrane.

STUART MEIKLEJOHN

June 1993

MEIKLEJOHN TAKES TITLE

At first glance, we may be fooled into thinking that this was just another tournament victory by Stuart - so familiar are we with his high level of successes over the years. How wrong could we be, this was a major Tournament victory, arguably the highlight of his career, when, in 1993, he triumphed against a very strong field to win the prestigeous East of Scotland title at Lundin Links.

The report continues:-

"Burntisland postie Stuart Meiklejohn put his annual leave to good use by winning the East of Scotland Open Amateur Championship at the weekend.

It was a first-class display from the 36 year old postman, who kept the prized title in Fife with a four over par aggregate score of 288 for the four rounds at Lundin Links.

The Aberdour Golf Club player stamped his authority on the tournament with a superb round on Sunday of 68 - one of only four sub par totals in the entire tournament and the lowest return of the weekend. His superb three under par round edged Meiklejohn two shots ahead of the overnight leader, Scottish Internationalist Craig Watson (East Renfrewshire) and early pacesetter Barclay Howard (Cochrane Castle).

A powerful westerly wind on Saturday dictated high scores. However, the picture changed when former professional Meiklejohn emerged on to the sun drenched course on Sunday. He dropped a shot at the opening hole but steadied himself with birdies at the 4th and 6th. He struck even better form on the inward nine with a birdie at the par 5 13th and two more at the 16th and 17th, while dropping just one stroke at the 11th.

Meiklejohn's final round was a little less steady, with bogies at the 4th, 6th, 8th, 16th and 18th and birdies at the 7th, 12th, 13th and 17th. But the Fifer kept his head as nearest rival Watson dropped crucial strokes. Challenges from other Scots cap Howard failed to materialise.

Afterwards Meiklejohn explained that his job involved working on every Saturday. He had taken his holidays to co-incide with the tournament, while managing to fit in just a couple of weekly practice rounds. He added that a defence of his title would depend on whether or not he could fit in the tournament with his holidays next year."

Best returns

Stuart Meiklejohn (Aberdour)	71	77	68	72	288
Craig Watson (East Renfrewshire)	75	70	73	73	291
Barclay Howard (Cochrane Castle)	70	76	74	72	292
Wilson Bryson (Drumpellier)	75	72	75	73	295
Neil Gemmell (Tantallon)	74	75	74	72	295

BRITISH BOYS' CHAMPIONSHIP 1965
A WEEK TO REMEMBER

"Aberdour boy wins top golfing honour", "Fine putting makes Milne Champion", "Fifer Milne holds on to win title", "Milne's short game gives him the title", "Milne shocks them all", "Graham (from the wee course that breeds Champions) takes the title".

These were just some of the headlines when, on Friday 20th August 1965, Graham Milne won the British Boys' Championship at Gullane, East Lothian.

After being eliminated in the first round of the Scottish Boys' Championship at North Berwick earlier in the year, Graham, despite having a good season up to that time, did not enter the Championship in the most confident of spirits. Match Play, however, as we all know, can be a strange game and requires a combination of mental toughness and a fair degree of golfing skill to be successful - especially playing up to two games a day over a period of 5 days.

After a steady start to his first round match, and aided by some fine iron play and putting, Graham won through by 1 hole. The second round again saw him take on an English opponent, and, after another close match in which the two players were only separated by a three hole winning burst from the 11th, Graham was victorious by 2/1.

As with all championships of this nature, the opponents never get any easier and in the 3rd round Graham was up against Lindsay Gordon who is still, to this day, a prominent Lothians golfer. Graham produced his best form of the week so far and triumphed, perhaps easier than expected, by 4/3.

Peter Moody, an English and British Internationalist, was Graham's next opponent. A formidable golfer and perhaps one of the outside favourites for the Championship. After some inspired golf, a 5/4 victory provided arguably the shock of the round.

The 5th round saw Graham up against Peter Dawson, a fine young left handed golfer from Ganton. This tie produced one of the best matches of the tournament with both players producing sub par golf. Graham, after being hit with a start of par, birdie, birdie from his talented opponent, found himself rather quickly 3 down. In typical fighting spirit, Graham held his nerve and in a run of 2 under to the 9th, won 5 out of the 6 holes to turn 2 up. Graham went 3 up with a birdie four at the 12th and, despite dropping no further shots to par, stood on the last tee only 1 up. Birdies at the 13th and 17th brought Dawson right back into the game and his confidence was high. When Dawson fired his second to 8 ft at the 18th the pressure was on but Graham responded with a fine approach to 14 ft. In went the putt, a half in birdie was conceded and Graham triumphed in an excellent match by 1 hole.

Bernard Gallacher and Peter Oosterhuis, among the favourites, were eliminated from the championship at this stage.

Jim Farmer, now a Professional golfer, was Graham's next opponent in the quarter final. The pressure on youngsters reaching the later stages of any tournament such as this is intense and the standard of golf was perhaps not as high as would be expected from such a quarter final match. At the 1st, Graham hit a poor second and found a horrible lie in a bunker. Farmer, safely on in two, was confident of going 1 up. However, a beautiful recovery bunker shot saw Graham hole out in birdie three to win a hole that did not appear possible a few moments earlier. Despite some indifferent golf, Graham went 2 up after 10 holes and held that advantage with 4 to play. Poor shots at the 15th and 16th found sand and the two holes lost meant that the match was now all square with two to play. A fine second shot to 5 ft at the 17th by Farmer should have brought a winning birdie but the putt, much to Graham's relief, slid agonisingly by the hole. The 18th was another nervous affair with Graham playing the hole badly and 8 ft away in three. Farmer, after a bunkered drive, played a glorious recovery and then chipped to 4 ft. Under extremely tense conditions, both player showed their mettle and holed tricky putts to take the match up the 19th. With both players hitting fine seconds to the first extra hole, it was Graham who holed the winning birdie putt to go through to a place in the semi final .

The line up for the semi finals matched Oliver Brizon, the French Champion against David Midgely who, like Graham, was fairly unknown at this level. Graham's opponent was the powerful Sinclair Ferguson, a Scottish Intenationalist and now hot favourite for the title.

Midgely, only 16, who had beaten the Scottish Champion in the previous round, did not appear to have the goods to beat the powerful Frenchman and found himself 3 down at the turn. However, fine golf over the inward nine levelled the match and, after 18 holes, the pair set off up the 19th. An uncharacteristically bad second shot by Brizon at the 19th was enough to see Midgely through to the final by virtue of a steady par 4 to Brizon's 5.

Graham's opponent, Sinclair Ferguson, who had beaten Billy Lockie from Troon in the previous round, was a formidable opponent. As if overawed by the occasion, Graham had a disastrous start of 5, 5, 6 and, if that wasn't bad enough, a 25 ft putt by Ferguson at the 7th saw Graham 3 down and things were not looking very good at all. This was not the first time that Graham had been in such a precarious position but the match took an unexpected turn after Graham hit two fine shots at the 8th for a winning birdie 3 which was quickly followed with another winning 3 at the 9th. The next four holes were halved and at the 14th a fine four by Graham was sufficient to square the match. The 15th, however, produced the shot of the match. Both players were short in two at this long par 5 and from 40 yards, Graham holed his pitch shot for a winning eagle 3. Graham, now 1 up with three to play, holed a nasty 10 ft putt at the 16th for a half and with solid pars at the 17th and 18th saw him through to a most unexpected final appearance against David Midgely from Todmorden, Yorkshire.

For the day of the final, the weather was bright but an extremely strong wind made conditions difficult for both competitors. Big crowds gathered, brief highlights of the match were to be shown on television and the press also required pictures to meet the early editions. It is safe to say that all this did not have the most settling of effects on the two finalists who were no doubt very nervous anyway.

And so to the final itself. The standard of golf was very good given the difficult conditions and considering what a traumatic experience the whole affair was for both players. Graham lost the first hole but a 3 yard winning putt at the 3rd squared the match. Even at this early point, it was the player who could hold his game together in the difficult conditions that would survive and it was Graham who took advantage of some indifferent shots by his opponent to turn 3 up. A great birdie into the teeth of the wind at the 10th saw Midgely reduce the deficit to 2 holes. A 3 yard putt at the 11th must have looked good for a further gain by Midgely but Graham calmly followed him in from a slightly shorter distance for a half. Graham then won the 12th, Midgely played a fantastic recovery shot at the 13th for an unlikely half, but then Graham forged ahead winning 3 of the next 4 holes. A half at the 18th saw Graham 6 up after the first 18 holes of the final.

As with all matches where a commanding lead has been established, it is sometimes better if you can keep playing and therefore keep the momentum going. However, the break for lunch seemed to change the pattern of the game and for the early part of the afternoon round Midgely took the game right back to Graham. A second shot to 3 ft at the 19th for a winning birdie three set the early tone and further successes at the 22nd and 29th saw Graham's lead reduced to 3 up with 6 to play.

However, a vital time in Graham's round, and perhaps a turning point of the game, came at the difficult 5th (their 23rd) where Graham secured a most unlikely half in 5. After visiting two bunkers and finishing 5 yards above the hole in 4, Graham holed the tricky downhiller for a half in 5 after Midgely took three from the edge of the green, finally holing, rather nervously from 4ft for a half at a hole he seemed certain to win.

Following a half at the 30th and 31st holes, Graham hit a superb 3 iron into a strong cross wind at the 32nd to secure a winning birdie 3 and return to 4 up with 4 to play. Midgely responded in tremendous fashion powering two shots on to the long par 5 33rd hole for a winning eagle 3 but a solid 3 at the 34th saw Graham triumph by 4/2.

Graham attributed his success to an instinctive judgement of distance, his putting and general short game which was first class throughout the week. In fact, in all matches, Graham did not 3 putt on any occasion over the 8 matches covering 153 holes - a skill naturally developed on the tricky greens at Aberdour.

Winning the British Boys' Championship in 1965 was a major achievement and a memory that will remain with Graham and Aberdour Golf Club for many, many years to come.

A Memorable Round

David Ritchie had been playing golf seriously for almost four years, having previously had only a holiday time relationship with various cut down hickory shafted clubs including a Mashie-niblick, Brassie Wood and a ladies' 5 iron, since Easter 1962.

Following a successful year as a junior in 1974 along with two others - Sandy Cunningham and Lance Sloan, David was invited to play in the Gents' Section. This enabled participation in the medals during the year. If unaccompanied by an adult member, the hours of play for junior members were restricted by the club constitution, junior members' play being permitted only at specific times on the course.

Midweek medals had been introduced by the Match Committee during the 1972/1973 season as a means of providing an extra scoring opportunity played on a Wednesday in each of the summer months. The Green Staff had to work that bit harder on a Wednesday Medal day, by cutting the greens early in the morning, and tidying up the fringes prior to the start of play.

Members were required to arrange their own starting time with another member of their choice. As both Sandy Cunningham and David had completed their examinations at secondary school, it seemed appropriate to enjoy themselves and to try to lower their handicaps by playing in the competition on 16th June 1976. Not knowing how significant a round it was going to be, they teed off following a number of retired golfing groups playing after lunchtime.

David's round started off quite consistently by hitting all of the first nine greens in regulation, and birdieing the short 5th hole (Wicket) from about six foot below the hole, other birdies coming at the 8th (Downings), and 9th (Oxcar) holes, to be out in 28 strokes. Birdies at the 10th (Cottage), and 11th (Ainsley's Pier) with a par 3 up the hill at the 12th (Heich) gave a five under par score for the first 12 holes.

This was a significant low score in a number of ways. David had not had four consecutive birdies in a medal previously, although the 27 strokes for nine holes from the 4th (Kinniker) to 12th (Heich) holes equalled his previous lowest score whilst playing as a junior over these holes. After good drives up the 13th (St Colme) both players took a short sup of some water from the ladle at Simpson's Well prior to completing the hole in par.

The Well hole no. 14 (Cauldback), created many hazards for one playing off the small rubber mat. Nevertheless David hit the green which was then surrounded by no less than eight bunkers. A good tricky downhill putt gave him a six under par score and more importantly a cushion for the next three holes along the Avenue. Barely managing to keep his composure, David recalls that the pressure began to build, knowing that there were only four holes to go and a course record was well within his sights.

Following a good drive on the 15th (Ash Tree) David's three wood second flew over the marker pole but landed well short and right of the green side bunkers. A cleanly hit pitch ran past the flag stopping towards the back of the green. Thereafter he negotiated his first single putt par - the first major difficulty was passed.

For once, doubts crept into David's mind on the tee. The right hand fairway bunker had on a previous occasion blighted his score when it caught his drive and had resulted in a double bogey. The pressure was beginning to build up inside. He was uncertain whether to go with the driver already in his hand or to change to an iron. David stated after his round that instinctively he considered it better to concentrate on hitting a full drive rather than laying up with an iron, thereby preferring to hit in a half wedge for his second to the green rather than holding back on a full tee shot where he knew greater error may exist.

Drawing on all his experience an adequate tee shot was hit just missing the fairway bunker. It was uncharacteristic of all the previous solidly hit shots up till then, yet probably as good as could have been expected when his concentration was straying on to the prospect of a course record.

David marched down the fairway anxious to see how good a lie he had in the rough bordering the right hand fairway. Somehow the half wedge shot that he had foreseen on the tee was now more challenging. It was for this reason that he decided to hit a 9 iron pitch to land two thirds of the way and run on to the green, rather than a full pitch up on to the green. If any doubts in his own ability had existed on the tee, these were rapidly erased with the gentle sound of the ball running into the cup for a birdie on his resultant fifteen footer cross-borrow putt (now - seven under par).

The weather was beginning to freshen. On the 17th tee, a normal 5 or 6 iron shot required to be reselected as a comfortable 4 or a solid 5 iron. The pin was on the right half centrally positioned. David hit the bolder 5 iron shot, only to come off the swing, his ball landing short and right of the first right bunker. Somehow he pitched a sweet sand iron up to within seven or eight feet of the hole and holed the putt to save his par 3 - his second par saving putt of the round.

Following this confidence boost, the Pavilion hole (no. 18) for once would hold no fears. A good drive down the wall of the tall sycamore and elm trees, followed by a cleanly hit 6 iron held up into the breeze, landed about twelve foot short and left of the pin. Concentrating so intensely, not even the noise of the car park distracting him from the task in hand. The first putt missed but only just, leaving a fifteen inch tap in for his par. In it went for a seven under par total of 56 and a new course record!

The two junior members wandered into Neil Mackintosh's shop to get another card to copy David's score. Sandy, his playing partner, was only too pleased to write out another copy of the card to give him as a keepsake. When they were asked how they had done by the members about to start their round, a couple of regulars were heard to say "well, there's no' much point going out now".

No doubt at all, after cycling home, David enjoyed the remainder of the week, reliving each shot over and over, hardly able to contain the pleasure in what he had achieved - 28 out, 28 in, 28 putts for a gross 56 (net - 52).

To this day David maintains that an understanding partner who does not distract or say anything untoward always assists in achieving a good score - *'A course record, all thanks to a courteous partner.'*

Course Record 16th June 1976

Hole	Name	Yards	Par	Score	Hole	Name	Yards	Par	Score
1	Bellhouse	145	3	3	10	Cottage	220	3	2
2	Firs	156	3	3	11	Ainsley's Pier	251	4	3
3	Roundal	197	3	3	12	Heich	134	3	3
4	Kinniker	355	4	4	13	St.Colme	376	4	4
5	Wicket	133	3	2	14	Cauldback	110	3	2
6	Manse	300	4	4	15	Ash Tree	456	4	4
7	Doocot	165	3	3	16	Avenue	314	4	3
8	Downings	255	4	3	17	Woodside	172	3	3
9	Oxcar	291	4	3	18	Pavilion	401	4	4
OUT		1997	31	28	IN		2434	32	28
					OUT		1997	31	28
Player :- David Ritchie					TOTAL		4431	63	56
Marker :- Sandy Cunningham					HANDICAP				4
s.s.s. 62 (Gents) 64 (Ladies)					NET SCORE				52

APPENDIX 1

CAPTAINS OF THE CLUB

1896-1915	Rev W H Gray
1915-1925	Rev J Brown
1925-1928	T Scott
1928-1930	Major E C Moubray
1930-1932	A S Kinnear
1932-1934	R R Gillon
1934-1936	A G Kirk
1936-1938	J G Jack
1938-1939	Comdr G De Wilton
1939-1947	J W W Kemp
1947-1949	R A Laing
1949-1951	J Bald Jr
1951-1953	R A Somervaille
1953-1955	C M Gibb
1955-1957	Surgeon Comdr R Russell
1957-1959	A H Balfour
1959-1961	Surgeon Comdr R Russell
1961-1963	W Pennycook
1963-1965	W P Armit
1965-1966	I H Stewart
1966-1968	W M Bald
1968-1970	W R Allan
1970-1972	R Christie
1972-1974	M Thomson
1974-1976	I Gram-Hansen
1976-1978	H A Hanlon
1978-1979	R M Walker
1979-1981	M R S Cunningham MBE
1981-1983	R Pearston
1983-1985	E N Marsh
1985-1987	A M Grant
1987-1989	T J Oliphant
1989-1991	G R Milne
1991-1993	I A Gray
1993-1995	R A Scott
1995	W M Crowe

APPENDIX 2

LADY CAPTAINS

1906-1910	Mrs J Oliver
1910-1913	Mrs E N Wishart
1913-1914	Mrs E N Douglas
1914-1923	Miss H M Somerville
1923-1925	Mrs E N Douglas
1925-1928	Mrs E W Kerr
1928-1929	Miss M E Nelson
1929-1930	Mrs M N T Grahame
1930-1932	Mrs E W Kerr
1932-1934	Miss C C Melville
1934-1936	Miss J Gillon
1936-1938	Mrs A E G Ferguson
1938-1949	Mrs E W Kerr
1949-1951	Mrs M Morris
1951-1952	Mrs E Machin
1952-1954	Mrs J J Sutherland
1954-1956	Mrs V M Stuart
1956-1958	Mrs E W Kerr
1958-1960	Miss J L Anderson
1960-1962	Miss B L Crichton
1962-1963	Mrs W Stuart
1963-1965	Miss J B Lawrence
1965-1967	Mrs M W Armit
1967-1969	Miss B L Crichton
1969-1971	Mrs M Hallissey
1971-1973	Miss J M Bald
1973-1975	Mrs L M Borthwick
1975-1977	Mrs J Y Eadie
1977-1979	Mrs R P Stuart
1979-1981	Mrs A F Milne
1981-1983	Mrs S W Marsh
1983-1985	Miss Y L Sloan
1985-1987	Mrs V K Milne
1987-1989	Mrs L E W Hutchison
1989-1991	Mrs H M Thomson
1991-1993	Mrs R H C Smith
1993-1995	Mrs D Andrews
1995	Miss J M Bald

APPENDIX 3

CLUB COMPETITIONS

THE CHALLENGE CUP

Aberdour Club Championship, for many years consisted of two rounds of strokeplay (scratch) with the first 8 qualifying for matchplay. The final was played over 36 holes. In 1976 the competition was changed to 72 holes strokeplay with the first 20 after 36 holes contesting the final 36 holes. The format was briefly changed to matchplay in the 1980s, reverting to strokeplay thereafter.

1906 D Leitch	1937 R F Cuthill	1969 G R Milne
1907 J Seath	1938 D MacKenzie	1970 G R Milne
1908 W Crow	1939 J B Bald	1971 G R Milne
1909 W S Crow	1940 J B Bald	1972 S Meiklejohn
1910 W E Crow	1944 J A Burnett	1973 G R Milne
1911 W Nelson	1946 W S Thomson	1974 D J Dible
1912 W S Crow	1947 D MacKenzie	1975 G R Milne
1913 W S Crow	1948 J Findlay	1976 A P Hubble
1914 W Craven	1949 W M Ogg	1977 A P Hubble
1915 D Nelson	1950 D MacKenzie	1978 A P Hubble
1919 Rev J Brown	1951 F Scott	1979 G R Milne
1920 W S Crow	1952 E A McRuvie	1980 D J Dible
1921 J Horne	1953 W M Ogg	1981 A P Hubble
1922 D Nelson	1954 W M Ogg	1982 A P Hubble
1923 D W Nelson	1955 W M Ogg	1983 J McGlynn
1924 W S Crow	1956 R Simpson	1984 A P Hubble
1925 J B Dow	1957 G M Colman	1985 S Meiklejohn
1926 J B Dow	1958 W M Ogg	1986 S Meiklejohn
1927 J Bald Jr.	1959 R L Simpson	1987 S Meiklejohn
1928 J Bald Jr.	1960 W M Ogg	1988 S Meiklejohn
1929 J F Williamson	1961 W M Ogg	1989 S Meiklejohn
1930 T Grahame	1962 B J Eldred	1990 S Meiklejohn
1931 R L Johnstone	1963 W M Ogg	1991 S Meiklejohn
1932 R F Cuthill	1964 W M Ogg	1992 S Meiklejohn
1933 R F Cuthill	1965 W M Ogg	1993 S Meiklejohn
1934 R L Johnstone	1966 G R Milne	1994 S Meiklejohn
1935 I Moyes	1967 A MacNaughton	1995 S Meiklejohn
1936 D W Nelson	1968 G R Milne	1996 S Meiklejohn

THE WALKER TROPHY

Presented to the Club by R M Walker in 1976. Scratch matchplay Championship restricted to members with single figure handicaps.

1976 T J Oliphant	1983 A P Hubble	1990 M G Taylor
1977 G R Milne	1984 S Meiklejohn	1991 D W R Miller
1978 A MacNaughton	1985 A McGlynn	1992 S Meiklejohn
1979 A Hubble	1986 A P Hubble	1993 S Meiklejohn
1980 B J Eldred	1987 S Meiklejohn	1994 A P Hubble
1981 A Hubble	1988 S Meiklejohn	1995 S Meiklejohn
1982 N Miller	1989 A P Hubble	1996 A P Hubble

THE ROLLAND MEDAL

The oldest Club trophy.

1898 Rev. John Brown	1931 J B Dow	1964 R Taylor
1899 Walter Crow	1932 R F Cuthill	1965 D Colman
1900 No Competition	1933 S J Atkinson	1966 J H Borthwick
1901 No Competition	1934 D Bald	1967 A McLeish
1902 No Competition	1935 W D Nelson	1968 H Connell
1903 No Competition	1936 J Dow	1969 W P Armit
1904 No Competition	1937 R P Laing	1970 J Y Eadie
1905 No Competition	1938 W S Thomson	1971 J L Kennedy
1906 No Competition	1939 V H Ure	1972 G Maclachlan
1907 J K McLeod	1940 W F Lorimer	1973 C Rae
1908 W S Crow	1941 No Competition	1974 W McRae
1909 W Craven	1942 No Competition	1975 J Robb
1910 Thos Millar	1943 No Competition	1976 R A P Armit
1911 R Herd	1944 No Competition	1977 J Tyler
1912 No Competition	1945 No Competition	1978 D Neilson
1913 No Competition	1946 No Competition	1979 I Carstairs
1914 No Competition	1947 J B Bald	1980 T Young
1915 No Competition	1948 P A Moir	1981 B Durkin
1916 No Competition	1949 W Ogg	1982 F Arthur
1917 No Competition	1950 C J Kerr	1983 M Thomson
1918 No Competition	1951 J A H Reid	1984 A McVay
1919 No Competition	1952 W Pennycook	1985 E A Rice
1920 No Competition	1953 A D McQueen	1986 W Wood
1921 No Competition	1954 Jack Bald	1987 C A C Gray
1922 No Competition	1955 J McLauchlan	1988 D Houston
1923 No Competition	1956 B Eldred	1989 R Pearston
1924 No Competition	1957 J Erskine	1990 W M Crowe
1925 No Competition	1958 K Hedderwick	1991 D Bisset
1926 No Competition	1959 A Alexander	1992 N Hill
1927 T Grahame	1960 A Armit	1993 P Stackhouse
1928 R Cuthill	1961 J Turnbull	1994 R Thomson
1929 R Cuthill	1962 E Wood	1995 C Thow
1930 J F Williamson	1963 L Moir	1996 W Bartley

THE HILLSIDE TROPHY

Presented in 1906 - Annual matchplay on handicap.

1906 John L Somerville	1941 W E Crow	1972 D Bisset
1907 H C Lyon	1942 Comdr C F Brittan	1973 Jack Bald
1908 W S Crow	1943 J B Stove	1974 B J Eldred
1909 W S Crow	1944 C Spiers	1975 R S Sloan
1910 W S Crow	1945 W Pennycook	1976 D Woolgar
1912 W S Crow	1946 W S Thomson	1977 C Clyde
1913 W S Crow	1947 R A Laing	1978 H Hanlon
1914 W E Crow	1948 J Findlay	1979 B Eldred
1915 W S Milburn	1949 C J Kerr	1980 I Gram-Hansen
1919 Jeffrey Gibb	1950 J Turnbull	1981 B Durkin
1920 D Neilson	1951 J Turnbull	1982 B Garrod
1921 J Bald	1952 J A H Reid	1983 C A Clyde
1922 Rev R Johnstone	1953 L Moir	1984 S Meiklejohn
1923 L Johnstone	1954 J Young	1985 C A C Gray
1924 L Johnstone	1955 W M Ogg	1986 C A Clyde
1925 L Johnstone	1956 R Simpson	1987 P Hempseed
1926 D W Nelson	1957 G M Colman	1988 A W M Kerr
1927 J B Bald	1958 W M Ogg	1989 G Hughes
1928 T Grahame	1959 A McLeish	1990 J M McGlynn
1929 G S Young	1960 B Eldred	1991 G Thow
1930 T Grahame	1961 W M Ogg	1992 N Hill
1931 I Moyes	1962 R Law	1993 J Y Pearston
1932 R L Johnstone	1963 B J Eldred	1994 P White
1933 R A Laing	1964 G R Milne	1995 D F Dawe
1934 I Moyes	1965 C MacConnachie	1996 D Ritchie
1935 J B Dow	1966 K S Campbell	
1936 R F Cuthill	1967 M Thomson	
1937 J B Bald	1968 M Thomson	
1938 T Duncan	1969 G R Milne	
1939 M Wynyard	1970 G M Murray	
1940 R P Laing	1971 C A Clyde	

THE HILLSON TROPHY

Presented to Aberdour Golf Club by Mr L S Hillson of the Woodside Hotel in 1955.
18 Hole bogey competition on handicap.

1955 R Hutson	1969 I H Stewart	1983 R G Murray
1956 A C A Alexander	1970 B Durkin	1984 R Thurogood
1957 J H Amos	1971 I H Stewart	1985 B Garrod
1958 K Campbell	1972 J H Borthwick	1986 A R Hutt
1959 A Armit	1973 E N Marsh	1987 W Twaddle
1960 R Colman	1974 A M Young	1988 D Slater
1961 B Eldred	1975 H Hanlon	1989 R C Johnston
1962 M B Bald	1976 W M Ogg	1990 H T Connell
1963 J Coull	1977 E N Marsh	1991 G A Allan
1964 R Colman	1978 M Thomson	1992 T D Gourdie
1965 R M Colman	1979 W Twaddle	1993 I A Watt
1966 J Reekie	1980 C A Wotherspoon	1994 R Grant
1967 I H Stewart	1981 B Durkin	1995 No Competition
1968 T Oliphant	1982 A R Hutt	1996 A L MacGregor

THE CAMERON TROPHY

Presented to the Club by Mr Cameron of the Woodside Hotel in 1929. For
matchplay on handicap.

1929 H Martin	1954 L Moir	1976 D Woolgar
1930 J B Bald	1955 J Young	1977 I Gram-Hansen
1931 T F Drysdale	1956 I Mitchell	1978 M Doidge
1932 J B Dow	1957 J Erskine	1979 J Wotherspoon
1933 D Reid	1958 D W Gunn	1980 A R Hutt
1934 T Duncan	1959 D S Moir	1981 D Miller
1935 J MacKenzie	1960 R Colman	1982 J Y Pearston
1936 R F Cuthill	1961 W M Ogg	1983 P Hempseed
1937 W F Lorimer	1962 R Law	1984 A A Barr
1938 F Beard	1963 R Law	1985 C A C Gray
1939 W E Crowe	1964 B J Eldred	1986 A P Hubble
1940 J Bald Jr	1965 E N Marsh	1987 A P Hubble
1942 W Pennycook	1966 R A P Armit	1988 P White
1944 J Findlay	1967 I H Stewart	1989 C A C Gray
1946 D Colman	1968 H Connell	1990 P Hempseed
1947 R A Laing	1969 T Oliphant	1991 P Smith
1948 J Findlay	1970 B J Eldred	1992 C A C Gray
1949 E Kirkham	1971 B Latimer	1993 A Hill
1950 A W Grego	1972 E N Marsh	1994 S Drever
1951 P A Moir	1973 D Moffat	1995 D J Ritchie
1952 G Colman	1974 W McRae	1996 A D McGlynn
1953 J Borthwick	1975 B Eldred	

THE HEWITT MEDAL

Presented by the Hon. W H Hewitt in 1906 as a scratch medal competition. Not played for 1912 - 1926. Re-introduced as a foursome competition in 1927. Eventually became the summer monthly medal awarded to the player with the lowest 4 round aggregate from 6 monthly medals on handicap.

1906 J K McLeod	1951 H C L Young	1974 C Lyon
1907 J K McLeod	1952 E H Kirkham	1975 D Bryce
1908 W E Crow	1953 N Williamson	1976 W M Ogg
1909 W E Crow	1954 W M Ogg	1977 T Fisher
1910 W Craven	1955 J Borthwick	1978 M McGlynn
1911 W S Crow	1956 D Black	1979 F M Farmer
1927 T Grahame & J Bald Jr	1957 G M Muir	1980 C A Wotherspoon
1928 H C Lyon & W D Blair	1958 J Mullen	1981 G Steel
1929 R Cuthill & C Gibb	1959 B Eldred	1982 D Miller
1930 R F Cuthill & J Bald Jr	1960 B Eldred	1983 R A Scott
1932 J B Bald & D Reid	1961 J Erskine	1984 S Meiklejohn
1933 E C Moubray & J Bald Jr	1962 R Law	1985 J H Rough
1934 T Duncan & T Grahame	1963 W M Ogg	1986 J K Hutchinson
1935 R F Cuthill	1964 W M Ogg	1987 G D MacNeil
1936 H V Manson	1965 W M Ogg	1988 W Cooch
1937 W M Bald	1966 K S Campbell	1989 C A C Gray
1938 A Blair	1967 A H Kerr	1990 M A Scott
1939 H R Whitehouse	1968 A Turner	1991 C Westgarth
1946 D A Gunn	1969 A Turner	1992 J Crichton
1947 R W Marshall	1970 J Reekie	1993 G Polland
1948 T N S Harrower	1971 A King	1994 W Twaddle
1949 G Nisbet	1972 D J Dible	1995 D Colman
1950 J Turnbull	1973 C Lyon	1996 G Polland

THE MOUBRAY CUP

Presented to the Club by Admiral and Major Moubray in 1928. Originally an 18 Hole qualifying round on handicap, with first 4 qualifying for matchplay stage, now eight qualifiers contest matchplay on unadjusted handicap.

1928 Jas C Aitken	1953 P A Moir	1975 Jack Bald
1929 H Omand	1954 J Young	1976 J Adamson
1930 R A Laing	1955 J M Gray	1977 I Malcolm
1931 J B Bald	1956 W M Ogg	1978 A A Henderson
1932 G S Young	1957 B Eldred	1979 A H Burt
1933 S J Atkinson	1958 J H Amos	1980 A R Hutt
1934 R A Laing	1959 J Gibson	1981 W Moyes
1935 J Bald Jr	1960 A Wotherspoon	1982 M Thomson
1936 C J Kerr	1961 J H Borthwick	1983 K Ramsay
1937 W S Thomson	1962 R Colman	1984 S Meiklejohn
1938 R A Laing	1963 W S Thomson	1985 G Thurogood
1939 W F Lorimer	1964 W M Ogg	1986 W C Kelly
1940 W M Thomson	1965 G R Milne	1987 G R Thurogood
1942 R A Somervaille	1966 R Archibald	1988 R Pearston
1943 A D McHaffie	1967 T Oliphant	1989 A A Barr
1946 W S Thomson	1968 A P J Baldwin	1990 J R Duncan
1947 J Bald Jr	1969 A Wotherspoon	1991 N G Adams
1948 T C C Russell	1970 J Gray	1992 S Drever
1949 P A Moir	1971 W D Lanier	1993 D C Anderson
1950 D McKenzie	1972 R A P Armit	1994 P White
1951 N Bull	1973 L Moir	1995 R Aikman
1952 H C L Young	1974 A D McQueen	1996 A D McGlynn

THE GRAND FLEET CUP

Presented by the officers of the Grand Fleet (1914-1919). Handicap Competition 18 holes medal qualifying round, with the first 8 qualify for matchplay.

1920 M G Milburn	1947 D MacKenzie	1973 W B Miller
1921 A Brown	1948 J Findlay	1974 W M Ogg
1922 B Robertson	1949 Jack Bald	1975 K F Gibb
1923 B Robertson	1950 J Turnbull	1976 J Cuthill
1924 B Robertson	1951 H C L Young	1977 J Johnston
1926 C Milburn	1952 J Turnbull	1978 Ron Colman
1927 J B Bald	1953 W B Bald	1979 A Saunderson
1928 J B Bald	1954 J Bowman	1980 K Ramsay
1929 J B Bald	1955 A D McQueen	1981 N Miller
1930 J F Willamson	1956 N S Landale	1982 D Miller
1931 R L Johnstone	1957 J Erskine	1983 A P Hubble
1932 J B Bald	1958 R L Simpson	1984 S Johnstone
1933 D Reid	1959 F Beard	1985 J Crichton
1934 W Nicholson	1960 B Eldred	1986 E Dey
1935 I Moyes	1961 W M Ogg	1987 J Crichton
1936 J McLaren	1962 R M Colman	1988 R S McNulty
1937 W E Crowe	1963 W M Ogg	1989 W C Kelly
1938 A Blair	1964 W S Thomson	1990 I Mann
1939 D C H Martin	1965 G D Sheperd	1991 D Houston
1940 J Bald Jnr	1966 A M Clark	1992 S Johnstone
1941 David Bell	1967 M Thomson	1993 O Polland
1942 J W W Kemp	1968 A McLeish	1994 P Stackhouse
1943 W Pennycook	1969 R Colman	1995 K Ramsay
1944 James Findlay	1970 W M Ogg	1996 J Wilson
1945 C Spiers	1971 G R Milne	
1946 W S Thomson	1972 G R Milne	

THE ALEXANDER OLIPHANT TROPHY

Donated by the Oliphant family as an all Winners Trophy contested by the season's medal bogey and stableford winners. 18 hole stroke competition on handicaps.

1988 G D MacNeil	1991 R Pearston	1994 B J Eldred
1989 D Moffat	1992 J H Rough	1995 T D Gourdie
1990 M P Izzi	1993 R A Scott	1996 C A C Gray

THE DAVID COLMAN TROPHY

Donated by David Colman, Senior, one of the Club's most senior members and whose family has been associated with the Club since the Second World War. 18 hole stableford competition on handicap.

1979 D White	1985 A Saunderson	1991 A N McLaren
1980 J G McGarrity	1986 Jas Wilson	1992 B Eldred
1981 D Crookston	1987 A P Hubble	1993 C Thow
1982 N Hill	1988 J Glen	1994 M A Laing
1983 W Hutchison	1989 D P Colman	1995 M McKee
1984 E Dey	1990 A N McLaren	1996 E A Rice

THE SPRING CUP

Original Spring Cup badly damaged and replaced by the Council in 1961. Records of winners prior to 1961 are not available. 18 hole stroke competition on handicap.

1961 J H Stewart	1973 D Gault	1985 I A Gray
1962 W S Thomson	1974 J Y Pearston	1986 P Halleran
1963 W G Martin	1975 I A Gray	1987 M G Hill
1964 W R Allan	1976 A M Grant	1988 M G Doidge
1965 A R Blackler	1977 D Colman Jnr	1989 E Dey
1966 P McGowan	1978 D Moffat	1990 M Izzi
1967 G R Milne	1979 C Clyde	1991 S McGlynn
1968 A Wotherspoon	1980 I M Malcolm	1992 A Morrison
1969 R Christie	1981 A R Hutt	1993 N McLaren
1970 J Hunter	1982 D Moffat	1994 J Lakie
1971 W M Ogg	1983 R W Henderson	1995 Alan Parker
1972 J Gordon	1984 R Thurogood	1996 K Russell

THE SUMMER CUP

Presented by Gordon McCallum, Professional, for 18 hole medal competition on handicap.

1993 J Young	1995 A L Parker
1994 A R Hutt	1996 M Izzi

THE MUIR SCRATCH MEDAL

Presented by C L Muir, Club Professional in 1970, for the best aggregate scratch score for 4 rounds from the 6 monthly medals (April to September).

1970 G R Milne	1979 B Eldred	1988 S Meiklejohn
1971 G R Milne	1980 D Miller	1989 A P Hubble
1972 D J Dible	1981 G Steel	1990 S Meiklejohn
1973 W M Ogg	1982 A P Hubble	1991 D J Ritchie
1974 G R Milne	1983 A P Hubble	1992 S Meiklejohn
1975 G R Milne	1984 S Meiklejohn	1993 N Hill
1976 W M Ogg	1985 S Meiklejohn	1994 N Hill
1977 G R Milne	1986 S Meiklejohn	1995 N Hill
1978 J A King	1987 S Meiklejohn	1996 N Hill

THE MACNAUGHTON TROPHY

Presented to Aberdour Golf Club by Mrs K MacNaughton in memory of her husband Angus, who died in 1993. 72 hole handicap competition played in conjunction with Club Championship.

1993 J Duncan	1995 S Johnson
1994 N Hill	1996 N Miller

THE ALLAN TROPHY

Presented by W R Allan, Club Captain 1968-1970, for a gents' handicap championship which was originally contested over 72 holes in conjunction with the club championship, but later played separately as a 72 hole competition. Now played as a 36 hole competition.

1980 K Ramsay	1986 R A Scott	1992 P White
1981 R Henderson	1987 P White	1993 J Glen
1982 D Ritchie	1988 L Thurogood	1994 W Moyes
1983 S Meiklejohn	1989 G R Milne	1995 F Pajak
1984 C Wilson	1990 G R Milne	1996 C A C Gray
1985 D W R Miller	1991 I D Brown	

THE DRYBURGH CUP

Gentlemen's foursome matchplay Competition on Handicap.

1973 D Moffat & J Hunter	1985 I Macintyre & M R Wood
1974 A M Young & I A Gray	1986 D W R Miller & D J Ritchie
1975 D Dible & S Meiklejohn	1987 N A Henderson & G R Milne
1976 M Thomson & A Wotherspoon	1988 G R Milne & N A Henderson
1977 D Gault & I Gram-Hansen	1989 R S Sloan & R L Sloan
1978 G R Milne & B Eldred	1990 R S Sloan & R L Sloan
1979 B Eldred & D Bryce	1991 W C Kelly & Jas Wilson
1980 B Eldred & D Bryce	1992 D J Ritchie & D W R Miller
1981 J Hempseed & P Hempseed	1993 J McGlynn & S McGlynn
1982 J Taddei & B Garrod	1994 M McGlynn & I Purslow
1983 J Bald & D Hanlon	1995 A McGregor & C Gray
1984 C Wilson & D Slater	1996 D J Ritchie & D W R Miller

THE FAMOUS GROUSE SHOTGUN FOURSOMES COMPETITION

Donated to Aberdour Golf Club by Matthew Gloag & Son Limited, Perth, for annual four ball foursome competition with a shotgun start.

1986 S Johnston & H T Lavery	1992 A Kerr & I Gram-Hansen
1987 M J McKee & J C McKee	1993 D Anderson & Doug Anderson
1988 D Moffat & M R Wood	1994 C A C Gray & A McGregor
1989 N McLaren & C Baird	1995 W Moyes & M Doidge
1990 J Etherington & J Crichton	1996 P Stackhouse & M Laing
1991 G Hughes & C Hughes	

THE BRETT TROPHY

Presented to Aberdour Golf Club by Brett Precision Components Limited in 1989 for Gentlemen's Summer Fourball Competition on handicap (each partnership to consist of a high and low handicap).

1989 J Crichton & D Levein	1993 A Mitchell & W Fairgrieve
1990 R Pearston & I Gram-Hansen	1994 T D Gourdie & O Polland
1991 J Scott & D Levein	1995 E Dey & E N Marsh
1992 W Bartley & N Hill	1996 G Cormack & E A Rice

THE VICTORY CUP

Purchased by the Club to commemorate the end of the First World War and as recognition of those young men of the Club who served in France and elsewhere. Originally an individual competition. Became a foursome competition in 1935 and finally in 1973 a greensome competition over 18 holes on handicap (.4 of highest - .6 of lowest).

1919 W E Crow
1920 B Robertson
1921 Surg. Comdr. J McDonald
1922 R Bald
1923 C J Kerr
1924 D Nelson
1925 G H Hood
1926 - No competition
1927 C J Kerr
1928 C S Young
1929 J Bald Jnr
1930 J F Williamson
1931 I Moyes
1932 J B Bald
1933 D Bald
1934 R P Laing
1935 R F Cuthill & I Moyes
1936 C A Alexander & R A Findlay
1937 R P Laing & R A Laing
1938 R F Cuthill & C S Kerr
1939 W M Thomson & W S Thomson
1940 D C H Martin & W H Young
1941 - No competition
1942 J B Bald & W E Crowe
1943 C J Kerr & C Spiers
1944 Comdr C F Brittain & C Spiers
1945 J Donaldson & C Spiers
1946 R A Laing & M L T Wynyard
1947 W Hood & D MacKenzie
1948 J Bald Jnr & J Findlay
1949 R A Laing & P A Moir
1950 M T L Wynyard & G M Colman
1951 W B Bald & Dr Douglas
1952 Eng. Cap. N J Clift R.N. & E S Spillard
1953 P A Moir & C MacKinnon
1954 Jack Bald & N Williamson
1955 D Blaik & J Steel
1956 J P Amos & I Mitchell
1957 R Colman & D Buchan
1958 B Eldred & D Gault

1959 K M Campbell & L Moir
1960 J Findlay & A Hutt
1961 A D McQueen & I M Stuart
1962 R A P Armit & E Wood
1963 W B Findlay & I M Stuart
1964 I McFadyen & W S Thomson
1965 R M Colman & R S Johnston
1966 W P Armit & I D Bald
1967 J Bald & I H Stewart
1968 J Horn & C Stark
1969 W R Allan & I McFadyen
1970 J C Dempster & H S Fulton
1971 B Latimer & L Moir
1972 L Moir & R Welsh
1973 R G Halliday & E A Murray
1974 D Gault & I Gram-Hansen
1975 I Dyce & I Grieve
1976 J McGarrity & H Kenny
1977 H Connell & E N Marsh
1978 J Cuthill & I Purslow
1979 M R S Cunningham & W B Miller
1980 G E Doidge & M Doidge
1981 W Hay & A Saunderson
1982 J Anderson & J Gray
1983 R A Scott & B Garrod
1984 I Purslow & M McGlynn
1985 J Colman & O McVay
1986 A Cruickshank & W Wood
1987 S Wilson & A Ellington
1988 M G McGlynn & I Purslow
1989 B Garrod & M A Scott
1990 J Etherington & J Crichton
1991 R A Scott & J Scott
1992 W Fyffe & D Levein
1993 P Barton & J Barton
1994 C Clyde & A Gibson
1995 M McGlynn & I Purslow
1996 T D Gourdie & B Drever

THE DON McQUEEN CUP

Presented by Mrs McQueen to Aberdour Golf Club in memory of her husband Don, a member for many years. A three club and putter competition for men aged 65 and over on date of Competition.

1989 D Colman (Sen)	1992 R G Halliday	1995 B Sangster
1990 A M Fyfe	1993 A Masson	1996 E B Mackay
1991 R Pearston	1994 R G Halliday	

THE CHARLES HAWKINS TROPHY

Presented to Aberdour Golf Club in 1982 by Mr R Hawkins in memory of his father, Charles, a former member. Awarded annually to the best placed Aberdour player in the Invitation Seniors Tournament.

1982 W A Fowler	1987 A M Fyfe	1992 Ron Colman
1983 I H Stewart	1988 H T Connell	1993 Ron Colman
1984 I Gram-Hansen	1989 J J Train	1994 G R Brown
1985 W S Turnbull	1990 J J Train	1995 Ron Colman
1986 J J Train	1991 H Hanlon	1996 I Gram-Hansen

THE VETERANS' TROPHY

Presented by Miss H M Somerville (Lady Captain 1914 -1923) in 1965. At the time a member for 60 years and the oldest lady member in the Club. Matchplay Handicap Competition for Gentlemen 60 and over.

1965 J Findlay	1976 J F MacLachlan	1987 J Hunter
1966 A McLeish	1977 D Colman	1988 W M P Sime
1967 J Findlay	1978 R Hawkshaw	1989 R S Sloan
1968 J Findlay	1979 R Welsh	1990 H A Hanlon
1969 J Findlay	1980 L Moir	1991 Dr R S Sloan
1970 J Bald	1981 W Crowe	1992 C A Clyde
1971 L Moir	1982 R G Halliday	1993 B Eldred
1972 L Moir	1983 J Hunter	1994 Robt Colman
1973 R Hawkshaw	1984 A Fyfe	1995 C A Clyde
1974 K F Gibb	1985 A Fyfe	1996 C A Clyde
1975 L Moir	1986 I M Malcolm	

THE MACROBERT THISTLE CUP

Presented to Aberdour Golf Club by the National Playing Fields Association in 1975 for the Winter Foursomes Competition which had been in existence since 1971 but without a trophy for the winners from 1971 -1974.

1975 D Dible & S Meiklejohn	1986 R Colman & G R Milne
1976 A H Burt & J Moxon	1987 A M Grant & R A Scott
1977 J A King & P Hempseed	1988 D C Mack & R W Thurogood
1978 D Moffat & J Hempseed	1989 B Eldred & D Gault
1979 J Cuthill & I Purslow	1990 R W & L Thurogood
1980 A MacNaughton & A Hubble	1991 W Bartley & W Moyes
1981 B Eldred & D Bryce	1992 J Crichton & J Etherington
1982 W S Adam & M J McKee	1993 G McNeil & S Drever
1983 B Eldred & T Fisher	1994 W Moyes & A R Hutt
1984 A R Hutt & M Doidge	1995 S Johnston & D Dawe
1985 C Wilson & D Slater	1996 A MacGregor & C A C Gray

MIXED COMPETITIONS

THE BRIMER CUP

Donated by Mr T Brimer, proprietor of the Aberdour Hotel. 18 hole mixed foursome competition on handicap.

1927 Miss M E Nelson & J Bald Jnr
1928 Mrs T Grahame & G S Young
1929 Miss N Kerr & G S Young
1930 Mrs Greedigan & G S Young
1931 Miss H Rogerson & G S Young
1932 Mrs H B Watt & R A Laing
1933 Miss K T Lyon & I Moyes
1934 Miss K T Lyon & I Moyes
1935 Miss M Nelson & W D Nelson
1936 Mrs Laing & Mr Laing
1937 Miss Mitchell & R F Cuthill
1938 Mrs Hamilton & A Blair
1939 Mr & Mrs C J Kerr
1940 Mr & Mrs Thomson
1941 Miss M E Proctor & J Bald Jnr
1942 Miss M Proctor & J Bald Jnr
1943 -1947 No Competition
1948 Mrs E Machin & T C C Russell
1949 Miss N Kirkham & E Kirkham
1950 No Competition
1951 Mrs Greig Milburn & J Bald Jr
1952 Miss B Crichton & C M Gibb
1953 Mrs H Dornan & D Simpson
1954 Mrs W Pennycook & E H Kirkham
1955 Mrs H Dornan & D Simpson
1956 Mrs Timson & D Blaik
1957 Miss M Gullen & G M Muir
1958 Miss M Robertson & J H Borthwick
1959 Mrs Timson & D S Moir
1960 Miss J B Lawrence & M S Scougall
1961 Miss J Bald & A Armit
1962 Miss J B Lawrence & R Colman
1963 Mrs Pennycook & J Findlay
1964 Mrs Machin & Cmdr K R Stubbs

1965 Miss Woolgar & Mr Woolgar
1966 Miss S Walker & R M Walker
1967 Miss E Scott &J Findlay
1968 Miss V Hunt & A Wotherspoon
1969 Miss C Johnstone & R Colman
1970 Mrs G Grant & W P Armit
1971 Miss L Reekie & J H Borthwick
1972 Mrs M Walker & W P Armit
1973 Mrs V Young & A M Young
1974 Miss N Hume & J D Binnie
1975 Mr & Mrs I Gram-Hansen
1976 Mr & Mrs J F Maclauchlan
1977 Mr & Mrs H Hanlon
1978 Mr & Mrs C Rae
1979 Mr & Mrs D White
1980 Mr & Mrs R M Walker
1981 Mr & Mrs R M Walker
1982 Mrs M Simpson & M Condie
1983 Mrs S Robb & M Thomson
1984 Mrs C Twaddle & W T Twaddle
1985 Mrs J W Lake & J Lake
1986 Mrs A McKay & W McKay
1987 Mrs A McKay & W McKay
1988 Mrs J Gunn & J K Dible
1989 Mr & Mrs R Pearston
1990 Mrs V Clyde & M A Scott
1991 Mrs W M Gibson & Dr G R Brown
1992 Mr & Mrs M R S Cunningham
1993 Mrs S Butler & R W Butler
1994 Mrs S Page & R Pearston
1995 Mrs E Rae & D Bisset
1996 Mrs K Laming & W Cochrane

THE TAPPIT HEN TROPHY

Presented to Aberdour Golf Club in 1982 by Mr G Malcolm Murray for a Family Foursomes Competition.

1982 Mr & Mrs P Ramsay
1983 Mr & Mrs W Hutchison
1984 R M Walker & Mrs S Page
1985 G R Thurogood & L W Thurogood
1986 R Pearston & J Y Pearston
1987 Mr & Mrs A M Grant
1988 D H Gault & S Jobes
1989 G Hughes& C Hughes

1990 G Hughes & C Hughes
1991 W Fyffe & P Fyffe
1992 A Hutt & A R Hutt
1993 J Rough & J Rough
1994 Mr & Mrs I Mallinson
1995 Mr & Mrs I Mallinson
1996 I McIntyre & D McIntyre

THE MIXED FOURSOMES TROPHY (W M BALD TROPHY)

Presented by Walter M Bald (Club Captain in 1966 - 1968) in 1967 for mixed foursomes matchplay competition on handicaps.

1967 Dr & Mrs R S Sloan	1982 Ron Colman & Miss J Lawrence
1968 R S Johnston & Miss J Bald	1983 N Miller & Miss J Clyde
1969 R Colman & Miss J B Lawrence	1984 D Gault & Mrs M Connelly
1970 R S Sloan & Miss Y Sloan	1985 G R Milne & Mrs V Milne
1971 R Christie & Miss M Woolgar	1986 B J Eldred & Miss E B Douglas
1972 R S Stewart & Miss C Simmers	1987 R S Sloan & Miss Y L Sloan
1973 G R Milne & Mrs V Milne	1988 W McKay & Mrs A McKay
1974 H Hanlon & Mrs A Hanlon	1989 G R Milne & Mrs V Milne
1975 A Wotherspoon & Mrs M Charles	1990 Dr R S Sloan & Miss Y L Sloan
1976 Mr & Mrs J F MacLachlan	1991 J H Rough & Mrs J Rough
1977 C Clyde & Mrs J Richardson	1992 G R Milne & Mrs V Milne
1978 Ron Colman & Miss J Lawrence	1993 W McKay & Mrs N McKay
1979 Dr R S Sloan & Miss Y Sloan	1994 A P Hubble & Mrs E Duff
1980 Ron Colman & Miss J Lawrence	1995 R A Scott & Mrs R A M Scott
1981 G M Murray & Miss J Bald	1996 I Dickson & Mrs F S Dickson

THE KAWED OOT CUP

Presented by A M Grant (Club Captain 1985-1987) and R A Scott (Club Captain 1993-1995) for annual handicap competition in mixed foursomes. Entry restricted to couples eliminated in the first round of the W M Bald mixed competition.

1991 B Eldred & Mrs M Spittal	1994 W E Heggie & Mrs M Hamilton
1992 B Garrod & Miss M Glennie	1995 A Grant & Mrs D Andrews
1993 R Pearston & Mrs S Page	1996 J Young & Mrs A F Milne

THE TYLER TROPHY

Presented to the Club in 1978 by John and Jayne Tyler, former members now resident in California. Mixed Greensome Competition on Handicap.

1978 Mr & Mrs T M Miller	1988 L W Thurogood & Mrs A Thurogood
1979 Mr & Mrs M R S Cunningham	1989 Mr & Mrs W D B Andrews
1980 C A Clyde & Mrs M Dawe	1990 D Gault & Mrs M Connolly
1981 Mr & Mrs R M Walker	1991 R Pearston & Mrs S Page
1982 Mr & Mrs A W Kerr	1992 Mr & Mrs M Wood
1983 D W R Miller & Miss P Pearston	1993 R A MacEachen & Mrs W Schumacher
1984 Mr & Mrs G Schumacher	1994 W A Heggie & Mrs M Hamilton
1985 D W R Miller & Miss J Whyte	1995 D C Anderson & Mrs B Anderson
1986 J W Lake & Mrs A Lake	1996 N McLaren & Mrs W Schumacher
1987 B Garrod & Miss M M Glennie	

APPENDIX 4

LADIES' COMPETITIONS

THE LADIES' CLUB CHAMPIONSHIP

The Ladies' Championship Trophy was presented in 1960 by Miss J B Lawrence and Mrs W Rowell for an 18 hole qualifying competition with the best 8 scratch scores qualifying for the matchplay stage.

1960 Miss J B Lawrence	1973 Miss J Bald	1986 Miss J Bald
1961 Miss J B Lawrence	1974 Miss J Bald	1987 Miss J Bald
1962 Miss J B Lawrence	1975 Miss J Bald	1988 Mrs V K Milne
1963 Miss J B Lawrence	1976 Miss J B Lawrence	1989 Mrs R Scott
1964 Miss J B Lawrence	1977 Miss J B Lawrence	1990 Mrs R Scott
1965 Miss J Bald	1978 Mrs J White	1991 Mrs R Scott
1966 Miss J B Lawrence	1979 Miss J Bald	1992 Miss Y L Sloan
1967 Miss J B Lawrence	1980 Miss J Bald	1993 Mrs R Scott
1968 Miss J B Lawrence	1981 Miss Y L Sloan	1994 Miss Y L Sloan
1969 Miss J B Lawrence	1982 Miss Y L Sloan	1995 Miss M Glennie
1970 Miss J B Lawrence	1983 Miss J Bald	1996 Mrs R Scott
1971 Miss J Bald	1984 Miss J Bald	
1972 Miss J Bald	1985 Miss Y L Sloan	

THE LADIES' CLUB TROPHY

Presented in 1929 for annual competition - matchplay on handicap.

1929 Mrs E W Kerr	1957 Miss J B Lawrence	1977 Miss J B Lawrence
1930 Miss D Smith	1958 Miss B Crichton	1978 Miss J Bald
1931 Mrs Logan	1959 Mrs W Pennycook	1979 Miss J Bald
1932 Miss J Gillon	1960 Miss B Crichton	1980 Miss J B Lawrence
1933 Mrs Hamilton	1961 Miss B Crichton	1981 Mrs V Milne
1934 Miss H M Somerville	1962 Mrs W Rowell	1982 Miss Y Sloan
1935 Miss J Gillon	1963 Mrs C Stewart	1983 Miss J B Lawrence
1936 Mrs Hamilton	1964 Mrs W Rowell	1984 Mrs V Milne
1937 Miss J Gillon	1965 Mrs B Wilson	1985 Mrs J Mann
1938 Mrs W M Thomson	1966 Miss J B Lawrence	1986 Miss M Glennie
1939 Miss S Mitchell	1967 Miss J B Lawrence	1987 Mrs V Clyde
1940 Miss Drysdale	1968 Miss J Bald	1988 Mrs D B R Cuthill
1949 Mrs E S Machin	1969 Miss J Bald	1989 Mrs R Scott
1950 Mrs E S Machin	1970 Mrs W Gibson	1990 Mrs R Scott
1951 Miss B Crichton	1971 Mrs R Timson	1991 Mrs D Andrews
1952 Miss J L Anderson	1972 Miss J B Lawrence	1992 Mrs S Marsh
1953 Mrs H Doran	1973 Miss R Dunsmuir	1993 Mrs A Mallinson
1954 Miss B Crichton	1974 Mrs M Charles	1994 Mrs N McKay
1955 Mrs W A Dunn	1975 Miss B Crichton	1995 Mrs S Page
1956 Miss J B Lawrence	1976 Miss J B Lawrence	1996 Dr S Farrar

THE LADIES' YEARLY CUP

Presented in 1906 for a matchplay handicap competition played throughout the year.

1906 Helen M Somerville	1937 Mrs Grahame	1968 Miss J B Lawrence
1907 Mrs Wm Moyes	1938 Miss S Mitchell	1969 Miss B Crichton
1908 Mrs J Oliver	1939 Helen M Somerville	1970 Miss J B Lawrence
1909 Miss C G Houston	1940 Miss J Gillon	1971 Miss B Crichton
1910 Miss C Drummond	1941 No Competition	1972 Mrs S Marsh
1911 Belle K Drysdale	1942 No Competition	1973 Mrs M Charles
1912 Cissy G Houston	1943 No Competition	1974 Mrs M Millar
1913 Helen M Somerville	1944 No Competition	1975 Mrs L Borthwick
1914 Helen M Somerville	1945 No Competition	1976 Miss J B Lawrence
1915 Monica Millar	1946 No Competition	1977 Miss B Crichton
1916 No Competition	1947 No Competition	1978 Miss E M C Scott
1917 No Competition	1948 No Competition	1979 Miss J Bald
1918 No Competition	1949 Mrs Greig Milburn	1980 Miss J Bald
1919 Agnes Lyon	1950 Mrs Greig Milburn	1981 Miss Y Sloan
1920 Belle K Drysdale	1951 Miss B Crichton	1982 Mrs J White
1921 Mollie E Nelson	1952 Mrs J L Gray	1983 Miss J Bald
1922 Mollie E Nelson	1953 Mrs H Dornan	1984 Miss J Bald
1923 C A Laurie	1954 Miss B Crichton	1985 Mrs S Marsh
1924 Mrs R H Deane	1955 Mrs R Timson	1986 Mrs V Milne
1925 Julia Gillon	1956 Miss J B Lawrence	1987 Mrs A McKay
1926 Mollie E Nelson	1957 Mrs J Y Eadie	1988 Mrs D B R Cuthill
1927 Mollie E Nelson	1958 Miss J B Lawrence	1989 Miss J Bald
1928 Mrs C J Kerr	1959 Mrs W Rowell	1990 Mrs E B Mackay
1929 Mollie E Nelson	1960 Mrs W Rowell	1991 Miss Y Sloan
1930 Miss J Gillon	1961 Miss J B Lawrence	1992 Mrs J Rough
1931 Miss J Gillon	1962 Miss J B Lawrence	1993 Mrs A Mallinson
1932 Mrs Logan	1963 Miss J Pitcher	1994 Mrs D Cuthill
1933 Mrs Martin	1964 Miss J B Lawrence	1995 Mrs R Scott
1934 Miss E S Rose	1965 Miss J Bald	1996 Mrs L Maxwell
1935 Mrs Hamilton	1966 Mrs R Timson	
1936 Miss V H Easton	1967 Mrs J Dempster	

THE McLEISH TROPHY

Presented for Senior Ladies by Mrs J McLeish

1966 Mrs A Rushton	1977 Miss B Crichton	1988 Mrs A F Milne
1967 Mrs H Armstrong	1978 Mrs E B Mackay	1989 Mrs D Andrews
1968 Miss B Crichton	1979 Mrs E B Mackay	1990 Mrs D Cuthill
1969 Miss B Crichton	1980 Miss B Crichton	1991 Mrs S Marsh
1970 Miss B Crichton	1981 Miss J B Lawrence	1992 Mrs S Marsh
1971 Mrs M Millar	1982 Miss J B Lawrence	1993 Mrs M Simpson
1972 Miss B Crichton	1983 Miss B Crichton	1994 Mrs L Hutchison
1973 Mrs M Millar	1984 Miss J B Lawrence	1995 Mrs H Thomson
1974 Miss B Crichton	1985 Mrs J Mann	1996 Mrs S Marsh
1975 Mrs M Millar	1986 Mrs S Marsh	
1976 Mrs G M McIntyre	1987 Mrs S Robb	

THE ANSTY CUP

Donated by Jo Cunningham in 1983, for ladies' winter singles' competition.

1983 Mrs J Cunningham	1988 Mrs V K Milne	1993 Mrs S Page
1984 Mrs H Thomson	1989 Mrs R H Smith	1994 Mrs A F Milne
1985 Mrs W Perrin	1990 Mrs E B MacKay	1995 Mrs H Thomson
1986 Mrs M Grant	1991 Mrs J Richardson	1996 Mrs D Andrews
1987 Mrs D Cuthill	1992 Mrs K Laming	

THE TARANSAY QUAICH

Presented to the ladies section 1992 by Helen Thomson (Lady Captain from 1989-1991). A handicap 36 hole stableford competition played over 2 separate rounds of 18 holes.

1992 Mrs S Page	1994 Mrs I Stuart	1996 Mrs L Maxwell
1993 Mrs V Milne	1995 Mrs I Hendrie	

THE KINNIKER SALVER

Presented by the Ladies' Section for the Bronze Championship for an 18 hole qualifying competition with the best eight scratch bronze scores qualifying for matchplay.

1985 Mrs J Mann	1989 Mrs J Mann	1993 Mrs D Andrews
1986 Miss J Whyte	1990 Mrs D Andrews	1994 Mrs A F Milne
1987 Mrs D Andrews	1991 Mrs L Hutchison	1995 Mrs N McKay
1988 Mrs L Hutchison	1992 Mrs A F Milne	1996 Mrs F Dickson

THE LADIES' HEWITT MEDAL

Presented by the Hon Mrs W Hewitt in 1906 as a scratch medal for ladies.
Changed to foursomes competition in 1929 - best nett score over 18 holes.

1906 L M Peters	1914 Miss H Somerville	1922 Mollie E Nelson
1907 Miss H Somerville	1915 Miss H Somerville	1923 Mollie E Nelson
1908 Mrs J Oliver	1916 No Competition	1924 Mollie E Nelson
1909 Miss E C Brown	1917 No Competition	1925 Mollie E Nelson
1910 Miss H Somerville	1918 No Competition	1926 Mollie E Nelson
1911 Miss H Somerville	1919 No Competition	1927 No Competition
1912 Miss H Somerville	1920 No Competition	1928 Mollie E Nelson
1913 Miss H Somerville	1921 Nettie M Drysdale	

1929 Julia Gillon & Miss K Lyon	1963 Mrs J McLeish & Miss J B Lawrence
1930 Mrs Moubray & Miss Gillon	1964 Mrs Cowie & Mrs Rowell
1931 Mrs DeWilton & Mrs T Grahame	1965 Mrs Rowell & Miss Leslie
1932 Miss E Rose & Miss D T Smith	1966 Miss J B Lawrence & Miss M Duncan
1933 Mrs Laing & Miss Gillon	1967 Mrs K Hallissey & Mrs R Timson
1934 Mrs Duncan & Miss C Melville	1968 Mrs M Condie & Mrs J Eadie
1935 Mrs Kerr & Miss S Melville	1969 Miss L Reekie & Mrs L Young
1936 Miss Rose & Mrs Kennedy	1970 Miss S McLeish & Miss J McNab
1937 Mrs Milburn & Mrs Hamilton	1971 Mrs J Dempster & Miss J Dickson
1938 Mrs Laing & Miss Gillon	1972 Mrs P Lanier & Mrs S Marsh
1939 Mrs C J Kerr & Mrs W M Thomson	1973 Mrs A F Milne & Mrs R Timson
1940 Mrs Kennedy & Mrs W M Thomson	1974 Mrs K Newton & Mrs S Marsh
1941 No Competition	1975 Mrs M Fisher & Mrs G Armit
1942 No Competition	1976 Mrs A Welsh & Mrs J Mann
1943 No Competition	1977 Mrs L Hutchison & Mrs J Tyler
1944 No Competition	1978 Miss D Connel & Mrs J Mann
1945 No Competition	1979 Mrs D Cuthill & Mrs R Hawkshaw
1946 No Competition	1980 Mrs A Hanlon & Mrs S Marsh
1947 No Competition	1981 Mrs M Grant & Mrs K Halliday
1948 Mrs Greig Milburn & Mrs Ian Moyes	1982 Mrs D Cuthill & Mrs R Stuart
1949 Mrs C J Kerr & Mrs P Moir	1983 Miss E Douglas & Mrs M Kerr
1950 Miss J L Anderson & Mrs W Pennycook	1984 Mrs J Gunn & Mrs N McKay
1951 Mrs Machin & Miss C Simmers	1985 Mrs M Adams & Mrs M Dawe
1952 Mrs J G Scott & Mrs J Young	1986 Mrs A Hanlon & Mrs D Andrews
1953 Miss B Crichton & Miss C Sim	1987 Mrs B Smith & Mrs S Marsh
1954 Mrs H Dornan & Mrs R W Stuart	1988 Mrs J Mann & Mrs M E Crawford
1955 Miss J L Anderson & Mrs I Stuart	1989 Mrs J Mann & Mrs J Richardson
1956 Miss M G MacMillan & Mrs J Lawler	1990 Mrs V Milne & Mrs M Fisher
1957 Mrs R Timson & Mrs K Craig	1991 Mrs W Gibson & Mrs R Scott
1958 Miss J B Lawrence & Mrs Wm Dunn	1992 Mrs A Thurogood & Mrs R Scott
1959 Mrs J Y Eadie & Mrs C Spiers	1993 Mrs H Thomson & Mrs M Adams
1960 Miss B Crichton & Miss J McNab	1994 Mrs K Laming & Mrs R Scott
1961 Mrs J Kerr & Miss M Gullen	1995 Mrs M Adams & Mrs I Stuart
1962 Miss J B Lawrence & Miss J Pitcher	1996 Mrs D Cuthill & Mrs F Dickson

THE LADIES' CLUB CUP

The oldest trophy in the Ladies' Section. 18 hole strokeplay on handicap.

1898 Mary M Orr	1932 Miss I T Johnstone	1968 Miss M Woolgar
1899 Grace Kellock	1933 Miss A G Ferguson	1969 Miss L Reekie
1901 Nettie Lyon	1934 Mrs Howell	1970 Miss J Dickson
1902 Mary M Orr	1935 Miss C C Melville	1971 Miss L Reekie
1903 Nettie Lyon	1936 Mrs K Y Hall	1972 Mrs M Condie
1904 Jessie Oliver	1937 Miss Gillon	1973 Mrs J Pearston
1905 Mary Fraser	1938 Miss C C Melville	1974 Mrs C M Millar
1906 Nettie Lyon	1939 Mrs C J Kerr	1975 Mrs M Binney
1907 Bessie Brown	1940 Miss H M Somerville	1976 Miss C Simmers
1908 Mary Downie	1946 Mrs C J Kerr	1977 Mrs J Pearston
1909 Mary Arnott	1950 Mrs P A Moir	1978 Miss C Meechan
1910 H Somerville	1951 Miss C Simmers	1979 Mrs L Hutchison
1911 J R Allan	1952 Mrs R W Stuart	1980 Miss J Crosbie
1912 Belle K Drysdale	1953 Miss C Simmers	1981 Mrs J M White
1913 Jessie S Wood	1954 Miss C Simmers	1982 Mrs C Miller
1914 Nellie Brown	1955 Mrs G Watt	1983 Mrs J Gunn
1915 H Somerville	1956 Miss J A Coutts	1984 Miss M Malcolm
1921 Nettie M Drysdale	1957 Mrs A McLeish	1985 Miss M Malcolm
1922 Maisie MacLean	1958 Mrs R R Law	1986 Miss M Glennie
1923 E N Douglas	1959 Mrs E W Kerr	1988 Mrs E Muir
1924 J R Allan	1960 Miss J Dickson	1989 Mrs N McKay
1925 Mollie Nelson	1961 Mrs O Pask	1990 Mrs J Mann
1926 Netta Peace	1962 Miss C Simmers	1991 Mrs R Scott
1927 Netta Peace	1963 Mrs E Kerr	1992 Mrs J Smith
1928 Julia Gillon	1964 Mrs Adamson	1993 Mrs E Duff
1929 Mrs M N T Grahame	1965 Miss M Woolgar	1994 Mrs N McKay
1930 Mrs Laing	1966 Miss J B Lawrence	1995 Mrs H Thomson
1931 Mrs J R Allan	1967 Miss J Gibson	1996 Dr S Farrar

THE INCHCOLM ROSEBOWL

Presented by Miss Jean Bald in 1979 (Lady Captain 1971-73 and 1995-96). A ladies' foursome competition, drawn partners, with matchplay throughout the year.

1979 Miss J Bald & Mrs S Hempseed	1988 Mrs V K Milne & Mrs C Muir
1980 Mrs J Dempster & Mrs J M White	1989 Miss J Bald & Mrs M Hamilton
1981 Miss J Bald & Mrs S Marsh	1990 Mrs R Scott & Mrs S Marsh
1982 Miss J Bald & Mrs J Dempster	1991 Mrs J Cunningham & Mrs D Andrews
1983 Mrs E B MacKay & Mrs W Perrin	1992 Mrs L Hutchison & Mrs R Scott
1984 Mrs D Cuthill & Mrs W Perrin	1993 Mrs A Mallinson & Mrs S Butler
1985 Mrs M Spittal & Miss M Glennie	1994 Mrs V Milne & Mrs S Page
1986 Miss Y L Sloan & Mrs B Smith	1995 Mrs I Stuart & Mrs A Mallinson
1987 Miss J Bald & Mrs J Mann	1996 Mrs W Schumacher & Mrs R Scott

THE JULIA GILLON SILVER CUP

Presented by Mrs Edmond Gillon to Aberdour Golf Club in memory of her daughter Julia, 15 April 1949. 18 Hole strokeplay competition on handicap.

1949 Miss C Reekie	1966 Mrs M Condie	1982 Mrs C L McKay
1950 Mrs C J Kerr	1967 Mrs Grandison	1983 Mrs V Clyde
1951 Mrs C J Kerr	1968 Miss V Hunt	1984 Mrs S Marsh
1952 Mrs R W Stuart	1969 Miss J MacNab	1985 Mrs J Gunn
1953 Mrs J Young	1970 Mrs M Condie	1986 Mrs S Travers
1954 Mrs P Moir	1971 Miss J MacNab	1987 Mrs J Richardson
1955 Miss C Simmers	1972 Mrs M Fisher	1988 Miss M Crawford
1956 Mrs J Young	1973 Mrs H Cowie	1989 Mrs J Richardson
1957 Mrs C Hutton	1974 Mrs L Hutchison	1990 Mrs D Cuthill
1959 Mrs R Timson	1975 Miss S McLeish	1991 Mrs S Page
1960 Mrs J Eadie	1976 Miss S McLeish	1992 Mrs R Scott
1961 Miss M Eunson	1977 Mrs C Mulhearn	1993 Miss L Anderson
1962 Miss M Inglis	1978 Miss C Meechan	1994 Mrs L Hutchison
1963 Mrs L J Stewart	1979 Miss Y Sloan	1995 Mrs L Maxwell
1964 Miss J Bald	1980 Mrs J Pearston	1996 Mrs S Page
1965 Mrs Grandison	1981 Mrs J Pearston	

APPENDIX 5

JUNIOR COMPETITIONS

THE YOUTHS' TROPHY

This first trophy for Junior Members was presented to the Club in 1937 by the Captain at that time, Mr J G Jack, in memory of David Tait Jack, killed in France on 29 June 1916. Strokeplay on handicap initially over 10 holes but 18 holes from 1982.

1937 J R C Affleck	1957 C S Finnie	1977 J I Thomson
1938 W Chalmers	1958 J Queen	1978 I J Mann
1939 E H Kirkham	1959 S Walker	1979 N Hill
1940 R Laird	1960 M Walker	1980 J McGlynn
1941 J E Todd	1961 J Findlay	1981 R Sheperd
1942 C Alexander	1962 K Dagger	1982 I Mann
1943 R Colman	1963 K Dagger	1983 S Fraser
1944 J Turnbull	1964 G MacGillivray	1984 A Hill
1945 D Colman Jnr	1965 R McKay	1985 M Taylor
1946 G Colman	1966 I Clark	1986 John Duncan
1947 W Bald	1967 I Clark	1987 J R Duncan
1948 W M Collins	1968 A K Raeburn	1988 S Jobes
1949 W Bald	1969 J Cowin	1989 S E McGlynn
1950 J V Sword	1970 G S Anderson	1990 R Scott
1951 R L Simpson	1971 A Hubble	1991 S Rennie
1952 V Robertson	1972 A Hubble	1992 R Scott
1953 J Gordon	1973 D Hanlon	1993 P Stackhouse
1954 E B Durkin	1974 J A King	1994 C Thomson
1955 D G Moir	1975 N Malcolm	1995 No winner
1956 H Young	1976 J King	1996 No winner

THE SCRATCH MEDAL

Presented in 1970 by Charlie L Muir, Club Professional, for Junior Members.

1970 D J Dible	1979 D Miller	1988 J McGlynn
1971 S Meiklejohn	1980 N Malcolm	1989 James Duncan
1972 A Hubble	1981 A MacGregor	1990 S McGlynn
1973 A Hubble	1982 S Drever	1991 No winner
1974 D J Ritchie	1983 I Mann	1992 No winner
1975 J King	1984 A McGlynn	1993 R Thomson
1976 J King	1985 W Cooch	1994 P Stackhouse
1977 D Miller	1986 W Cooch	1995 No winner
1978 D Miller	1987 M Taylor	1996 No winner

THE WHITEHOUSE TROPHY

Presented by the family of Eng. Comdr. Holly Whitehouse R.N. who lost his life during the second world war. Stroke Competition on handicap.

1945 A F Sutcliffe	1963 Alan E Wrench	1981 M Murray
1946 G Colman	1964 Stuart Oliphant	1982 R Sheperd
1947 A Alexander	1965 J Wotherspoon	1983 R Dey
1948 J Turnbull	1966 A K Raeburn	1984 J Hill
1949 V Robinson	1967 Vivien Hunt	1985 W Cooch
1950 A Alexander	1968 R L Sloan	1986 C Hughes
1951 V Robertson	1969 I Dewar	1987 D R Anderson
1952 A Alexander	1970 J Pearston	1988 Jas Duncan
1953 R Stirling	1971 K McGarrity	1989 S E McGlynn
1954 I Rule	1972 D Hanlon	1990 R A Scott
1955 C P A Levein	1973 D Bald	1991 C Thow
1956 Charlotte S Finnie	1974 R L Sloan	1992 P Stackhouse
1957 J V D Reid	1975 V Gram-Hansen	1993 C Thow
1958 Alan Armit	1976 N Miller	1994 C Thomson
1959 Martin Bald	1977 I Mann	1995 No winner
1960 Ian McAndie	1978 Susan Chalmers	1996 C McKinnon
1961 C Wotherspoon	1979 N Southgate	
1962 Sheila Walker	1980 I Mann	

THE KIRKHAM CUP
MATCHPLAY CHAMPIONSHIP

Presented by Eric H Kirkham, former member and Club Professional for Junior Members originally as Matchplay Championship but now matchplay on handicap.

1963 C R Richards	1975 P McNair	1987 I R McKee
1964 C R Richards	1976 D Bald	1988 D Anderson
1965 No winner	1977 N Miller	1989 K Wilson
1966 G MacGillivray	1978 D Miller	1990 R A Scott
1967 A K Raeburn	1979 A MacGregor	1991 C R Hughes
1968 I Clark	1980 N Malcolm	1992 R Scott
1969 I Dewar	1981 A MacGregor	1993 F Munro
1970 S Meiklejohn	1982 W Heggie	1994 No winner
1971 D Wright	1983 M Taylor	1995 No winner
1972 A Cunningham	1984 M Taylor	1996 No winner
1973 D Slater	1985 A McKee	
1974 P Hempseed	1986 A Syme	

THE CHRISTOPHER JOBES MEMORIAL TROPHY

Presented by Mrs J Jobes in memory of her son Christopher, a junior member of the Club.

1990 D Anderson & S E McGlynn	1994 G Hunter & C McKinnon
1991 R Scott	1995 No winner
1992 A Wilson	1996 No winner
1993 G Thomson & G Hunter	

THE McPHERSON TROPHY

Presented to Aberdour Golf Club by McPherson Associates for a Junior Scratch Matchplay Competition.

1982 J McGlynn	1987 M Taylor	1992 R Scott
1983 A McGlynn	1988 M Taylor	1993 R Scott
1984 R Shepherd	1989 S E McGlynn	1994 No winner
1985 A McGlynn	1990 J M McGlynn	1995 No winner
1986 A D McGlynn	1991 J McGlynn	1996 No winner

THE ABERDOUR JUNIOR GOLF CUP   (PENNYCOOK CUP)

Presented in 1960 by W Pennycook, Club Captain 1961-1963.

1960 Sheila Walker	1973 B M Sloan	1986 C Hughes
1961 John Lyon	1974 D J Ritchie	1987 J Scott
1962 Timothy Oliphant	1975 G Steel	1988 Jas Duncan
1963 Graham Milne	1976 N Twaddle	1989 J Scott
1964 Hamish McArthur	1977 H Purslow	1990 S E McGlynn
1965 Michael Clark	1978 A MacGregor	1991 A Fyfe
1966 G McGillivray	1979 C Gray	1992 R Scott
1967 Susan Adamson	1980 N Malcolm	1993 R Thomson
1968 A K Raeburn	1981 A MacGregor	1994 R Thomson
1969 I Clark	1982 E Dey	1995 No winner
1970 M Paton	1983 Miss M Malcolm	1996 No winner
1971 S Meiklejohn	1984 M Taylor	
1972 A Hubble	1985 J McGlynn	

THE ROBERT TAYLOR JUNIOR TROPHY

1989 J Duncan	1992 R Scott	1995 No winner
1990 J R Duncan	1993 C Thow	1996 No winner
1991 S McGlynn	1994 Ross Thomson	

THE C L MUIR SHIELD

Presented by Charlie Muir, Club Professional in 1971. Junior Scratch Match Play Competition played over the summer season. Discontinued in 1987.

1971 D Dible	1977 D MacKenzie	1984 A McGlynn
1972 J Y Pearston	1979 N Miller	1985 C Hughes
1973 A Hubble	1980 N Miller	1986 J McGlynn
1974 D J Ritchie	1981 N Miller	1987 M Taylor
1975 P Hempseed	1982 J McGlynn	
1976 J King	1983 S Drever	

THE S G CUNNINGHAM MEDAL

Presented to the Club in 1994 by the Cunningham family.

1994 S Rennie	1995 No winner	1996 No winner

APPENDIX 6

Achievements at National and County Level of Aberdour Junior Members

NATIONAL LEVEL

1965	British Boys' Amateur Championship at Gullane	Winner - G Milne
1973	British Boys' Amateur Championship at Blairgowrie	Semi-finalist - D Dible
1973	English Boys' Internationalist Cap at Blairgowrie	D Dible
1974	Scottish Boys' Internationalist Reserve	S Meiklejohn

COUNTY AND DISTRICT LEVEL   (INDIVIDUAL)

1962	Fife Boys' Strokeplay Champion	G Milne
1965	Midland District Boys' Champion	G Milne
1971	Fife Boys' Strokeplay Champion (under 15)	D Dible
1974	Fife Boys' Matchplay Champion (under 18)	S Meiklejohn
1975	Fife Boys' Strokeplay Champion (under 18)	D Ritchie
1976	Fife Boys' Matchplay Champion (under 18)	D Ritchie
1977	Fife Boys' Strokeplay Champion (under 18)	J King
1978	Fife Boys' Strokeplay Champion (under 18)	J King
1978	Fife Boys' Matchplay Champion (under 18)	J King
1980	Fife Boys' Strokeplay Champion (under 16)	N Miller

COUNTY LEVEL (TEAM COMPETITION)

1972 Fife Boys' Team Champions
D Dible, S Meiklejohn, A K Raeburn, J Pearston
1973 Fife Boys' Team Champions
D Dible, S Meiklejohn, J Pearston,   I Clark
1974 Fife Boys' Team Champions
D Dible, S Meiklejohn, A Hubble, D Ritchie
1975 Fife Boys' Team Champions
S Cunningham, A Hubble, D Ritchie, R L Sloan
1976 Fife Boys' Team Champions
S Cunningham, A Hubble, D Ritchie, R L Sloan
1981 Fife Boys' Team Champions
G Steel, N Malcolm, M MacPhee, J McGlynn
1982 Fife Boys' Team Champions
N Miller, J McGlynn, M MacPhee, G Steel

District Inter-Club (Team Competitions)
Under 17 Kingsway Foursomes Winter League - Representatives

1979	1980	1981	1982	1983
D Miller	N Miller	N Miller	M Burt	J McGlynn
N Miller	G Steel	G Steel	S Drever	A McGlynn
N Malcolm	N Hill	N Hill	K Meiklejohn	M Burt
D MacKenzie	N Malcolm	N Malcolm	A McGlynn	I Mann
M MacPhee	M MacPhee	M MacPhee	J McGlynn	S Drever
G Steel	N Twaddle	J McGlynn	A MacGregor	S Johnson
N Twaddle	D MacKenzie	A MacGregor	R Shepherd	A McKee

APPENDIX 7

Achievements at National and County Level of Gentlemen Aberdour Members

National Level (Individual)

1993	East of Scotland Championship	S Meiklejohn
1994	Leven Gold Medal - Runner up	S Meiklejohn

County and District Level (Individual)

1960	Fife Amateur Matchplay Championship	W Ogg
1970	Fife Amateur Matchplay Championship	G Milne
1974	Fife Amateur Matchplay Championship	A MacNaughton
1987	Fife Amateur Strokeplay Championship	S Meiklejohn
1991	Fife Amateur Matchplay Championship	S Meiklejohn
1994	Fife Amateur Matchplay Championship	S Meiklejohn
1988	Fife Club Champion of Champions	S Meiklejohn
1989	Fife Club Champion of Champions	S Meiklejohn
1991	Fife Club Champion of Champions	S Meiklejohn
1996	Fife Club Champion of Champions	S Meiklejohn
1981	Fife Order of Merit 'MacKay Bowl'	A Hubble
1988	Fife Order of Merit 'MacKay Bowl'	S Meiklejohn
1989	Fife Order of Merit 'MacKay Bowl'	S Meiklejohn
1990	Fife Order of Merit 'MacKay Bowl'	S Meiklejohn
1991	Fife Order of Merit 'MacKay Bowl'	S Meiklejohn
1992	Fife Order of Merit 'MacKay Bowl'	S Meiklejohn
1993	Fife Order of Merit 'MacKay Bowl'	S Meiklejohn
1994	Fife Order of Merit 'MacKay Bowl'	S Meiklejohn
1995	Fife Order of Merit 'MacKay Bowl'	S Meiklejohn
1996	Fife Order of Merit 'MacKay Bowl'	S Meiklejohn
1988	Fife Amateur Youths' Matchplay Championship	M Taylor

County and District Level (Team Competition)

1984 Fife Team Championship
      G Milne, A Hubble, N Miller, N Hill
1985 Fife Team Championship
      S Meiklejohn, G Milne, A. Hubble, D Miller

1950   Fifeshire Advertiser Cup
       W Ogg, D Mackenzie, E Kirkham, J Findlay
1968   Fifeshire Advertiser Cup
       W Ogg, G Milne, R S Sloan, A MacNaughton
1971   Fifeshire Advertiser Cup
       R Colman, R A P Armit, A MacNaughton, G M Murray
1973   Fifeshire Advertiser Cup
       D Dible, S Meiklejohn, G Milne, A MacNaughton
1986   Fifeshire Advertiser Cup
       N Miller, D Miller, S Meiklejohn, A Hubble
1987   Fifeshire Advertiser Cup
       C Gray, A Hubble, S Meiklejohn, D Miller

1967   Nairn Trophy
       W Ogg, A MacNaughton, B Eldred, R Colman
1972   Nairn Trophy
       D Dible, S Meiklejohn, G Milne, W Ogg
1978   Nairn Trophy
       B Eldred, A. Hubble, A MacNaughton, G Milne
1982   Nairn Trophy
       B Eldred, R Colman, D Ritchie, D Miller
1985   Nairn Trophy
       S Meiklejohn, D Miller, J Pearston, C Gray
1986   Nairn Trophy
       S Meiklejohn,G Milne, D Miller, A Hubble
1991   Nairn Trophy
       S Meiklejohn, A Hubble, B Eldred, C Gray

1986/87   McIntosh Winter League (Scratch)
1986/87   McIntosh Winter League (Handicap)

APPENDIX 8

Achievements at National and County Level of Aberdour Ladies' Members

National Level

1964	East of Scotland Champion	Babs Crichton
1965	East of Scotland Champion	Jean Bald
1971	East of Scotland Champion	Joan B. Lawrence
1972	East of Scotland Champion	Joan B. Lawrence
1973	East of Scotland Champion	Jean Bald
1982	East of Scotland Champion	Jean Bald
1962	Scottish Champion	Joan B. Lawrence
1963	Scottish Champion	Joan B. Lawrence
1964	Scottish Champion	Joan B. Lawrence
1965	Scottish Championship - Runner up	Joan B. Lawrence
1964	Curtis Cup Internationalist	Joan B. Lawrence
1964	Espirito Santo Team	Joan B. Lawrence
1963	Vagliano Trophy Match	Joan B. Lawrence
1965	Vagliano Trophy Match	Joan B. Lawrence
1959	Scottish Internationalist	Joan B. Lawrence
1960	Scottish Internationalist	Joan B. Lawrence
1961	Scottish Internationalist	Joan B. Lawrence
1962	Scottish Internationalist	Joan B. Lawrence
1963	Scottish Internationalist	Joan B. Lawrence
1964	Scottish Internationalist	Joan B. Lawrence
1965	Scottish Internationalist	Joan B. Lawrence
1966	Scottish Internationalist	Joan B. Lawrence
1967	Scottish Internationalist	Joan B. Lawrence
1968	Scottish Internationalist	Joan B. Lawrence
1969	Scottish Internationalist	Joan B. Lawrence
1970	Scottish Internationalist	Joan B. Lawrence
1968	Scottish Internationalist	Jean Bald
1969	Scottish Internationalist	Jean Bald
1971	Scottish Internationalist	Jean Bald
1977	Scottish Veterans Champion	Babs Crichton
1982	Scottish Veterans Champion	Joan B. Lawrence
1983	Scottish Veterans Champion	Joan B. Lawrence
1984	Scottish Veterans Champion	Joan B. Lawrence
1975	Scottish Foursomes (Glasgow Evening Times Trophy)	Jean Bald & Yvonne Sloan
1982	Scottish Foursomes (Glasgow Evening Times Trophy)	Jean Bald & Yvonne Sloan
1965	European Team Championship	Joan B. Lawrence
1967	European Team Championship	Joan B. Lawrence
1969	European Team Championship	Joan B. Lawrence

1969	European Team Championship	Jean Bald
1971	British Team - Commonwealth Team Championship	Joan B. Lawrence - Ladies Captain
1985	European Team Championship	Jean Bald - Scottish Ladies Captain
1992	European Team Championship	Jean Bald - Scottish Ladies Captain
1973	LGU International Selector	Joan B. Lawrence
1974	LGU International Selector	Joan B. Lawrence
1975	LGU International Selector	Joan B. Lawrence
1976	LGU International Selector	Joan B. Lawrence
1980	LGU International Selector	Joan B. Lawrence
1981	LGU International Selector	Joan B. Lawrence
1982	LGU International Selector	Joan B. Lawrence
1983	LGU International Selector	Joan B. Lawrence
1988-92	LGU International Selector	Jean Bald
1989	LGU Chairman	Joan B. Lawrence
1996	FCLGA President	Joan B. Lawrence
1995-1997	SLGA President	Joan B. Lawrence
1995	LGU Councillor	Jean Bald

County and District Level

1953	Fife Champion	Joan B. Lawrence
1957 - to 1965	Fife Champion	Joan B. Lawrence
1966	Fife Champion	Jean Bald
1967	Fife Champion	Joan B. Lawrence
1968	Fife Champion	Joan B. Lawrence
1969	Fife Champion	Joan B. Lawrence
1970	Fife Champion	Jean Bald
1971	Fife Champion	Jean Bald
1973	Fife Champion	Jean Bald
1979	Fife Champion	Jean Bald
1981	Fife Champion	Jean Bald
1982	Fife Champion	Jean Bald
1983	Fife Champion	Rosemary Scott
1988	Fife Champion	Joan B. Lawrence
1990	Fife Champion	Joan B. Lawrence
1987	The Maitland Mackie Cup	M Morrison, C Miller, J Dempster, L Hutchison, J Whyte, H Cowie, N McKay, W Perrin

APPENDIX 9

CENTENARY COMPETITIONS

PROFESSIONAL AMATEUR TOURNAMENT
Sunday 28 April 1996

TEAM SCORES

	Team Score	Professional	Aberdour Team
1st (bih)	120	D Thomson	S Farrar, G Polland, J Thomson, I Watt, G Hughes, C Gray
2nd	120	S Thompson	B Mackay, A Cruickshank, W Rennie, M Scott, Ron Scott, P Stackhouse
3rd (bih)	123	C Gillies	N Milne, A Ellington, N Hill, R Grant, M Wood, W Bartley

Other Scores

	123	I. Young, B. Smith, W. R Allan, W. Fyffe, A. McLaren, D. Cuthill, D. Ritchie
	125	L. Vannet, I. Stuart, C. Munn, J. S. Anderson, G. Birse, D. Houston, C. Thow
	125	R. Weir, K. Laming, G. Cormack, J.W. Anderson, Les Wilson, M. Dowling, N. Henderson
	126	D. Robinson, Rosie Scott, D. Graham, M. McGlynn, M. McKee, J. Cameron, A. Hutt
	126	G. Weir, J. Bald, M. Laing, W. Twaddle, D. Levein, Sheila Robb, W. Crowe
	127	A. Tait, D. Andrews, P. White, S. Robb, H. Hanlon, A. McGlynn, W. C. Kelly
	128	F. Mann, M. Crawford, S. Wilson, P. Barton, R. Aikman, Richard Scott, R. Goodale
	128	A. Crerar, M. Grant, I. MacDonald, M. Izzi, B. Munro, E. B. Mackay, J. Young
	137	G. McCallum, Lois Wilson, E. Gerraghty, D. Cook jnr, I. Purslow, J. Glen, A. Grant

PROFESSIONAL SCORES

66	C. Gillies	Falkirk
67	S. Thompson	Gleddoch
67	A. Crerar	Downfield
67	I. Young	Braid Hills
68	R. Weir	Cowal
68	A. Tait	Cawder
68	G. Weir	Braid Hills
68	D. Thomson	Kings Links
70	L. Vannet	Carnoustie
71	F. Mann	Musselburgh
71	D. Robinson	Fereneze
77	G. McCallum	Aberdour

SPECIALS

Closest to Hole at 1st - B.Munro, E. B. Mackay, J. Young

Closest to hole at 7th - N. Hill, N. Milne, A. Ellington

Closest to hole at 2nd - A. Tait, Cawder

Stamina Prize - G. McCallum, Lois Wilson, E. Gerraghty, D. Cook jnr, I. Purslow, J. Glen, A. Grant

CENTENARY GAMBLERS COMPETITION
Saturday 25 May 1997

	Team	Total
1st	I. Watt, W. Crowe, W. Cross, I. MacDonald	£4,890
2nd	A. Hubble, N. Henderson, I. Dickson, G. Milne	£4,500
3rd	G. McNeil, S. Drever, J. Lakie, Alec Parker	£4,140

Other Scores

Ron Scott, A. Grant, P. White, G. Cormack	£4,110
K. Ramsay, I. Mallinson, A. Mallinson, I. McIntyre	£3,660
I. Purslow, D. Anderson, W. Adam, W. Cochrane	£3,570
G. Polland, O. Polland, R. Maceachen, R. Grant	£2,820
A. McLaren, B. Durkin, A. Seaton, R. McNulty	£2,700
C. Gray, A. McGregor, D. Dawe, S. Johnston	£2,640
G. Hughes, C. Hughes, W. Rennie, B. Drever	£2,490
W. Mackay, T. McIntyre, P. Halleron, J. Stafford	£2,040
J. Johnston, B. Eldred, D. Bisset, T. Ward	£2,040
W. Bartley, J. O'Brien, D. Gault, M. Wood	£1,640
W. Twaddle, L. Wilson, S. Wilson, A. Ellington	£1,590
P. Stackhouse, C. Thow, G. Thow, J. Taddei	£1,410
Rosie Scott, N. Milne, D. Cuthill, S. Marsh	£ 960
W. Galloway, Alan Parker, D. Levein, W. Fyffe	£ 300
N. Marsh, R. Pearston, W. Hutchison, H. Hanlon	"Bankrupt"

CENTENARY WEEK MIXED FOURSOMES COMPETITION
Sunday 16 June 1996

Foursomes Team	Score	
A Laing & L Hutchison	45.0	Winners
L Wahlroos & Betty Mackay	45.7	Runner up

Other Scores

Stan Wilson & D Campbell	46.0	
Ron Scott & Sheila Robb	47.0	
R Chorley & C Senior	47.7	
C Neilson & Rosie Scott	48.0	
W Twaddle & E Ramsay	48.3	
Stan Robb & B Crichton	48.3	
R G Halliday & B Smith	49.7	
T Chorley & D Andrews	50.3	
M Dowling & R M Wahlroos	50.3	
R Adams & C Miller	51.3	
L Wilson & J Lawrence	51.3	
W Crowe & N Milne	52.0	
K Halliday & M Laing	52.0	
J Train & F Dickson	52.3	
J Cameron & A Mirrey	52.3	
C Twaddle & M Adams	57.0	
W Hutchison & J Bald	60.0	

LADIES INVITATIONAL TEAM COMPETITION
Monday 17 June 1996

INVITATIONAL RESULTS
(Best 3 scores out of 4)

CLUB	SCORE	
Kirkcaldy	220	Winners
Dunfermline	238	Runner up

Other Scores

Pitreavie	244
Milnathort	244
Kinghorn	245
Burntisland	247
Dunnikier	249
Canmore	253
Edzell	257
Balbirnie	261

ABERDOUR RESULTS

Aberdour 5	214	Winners

(Irene Stuart, Margaret Steele,
Marjorie Crawford and Sheila Robb)

Other Scores

Aberdour 4	219
Aberdour 3	222
Aberdour 2	227
Aberdour 1	228

SENIOR MEMBERS COMPETITION

SENIORS CENTENARY CUP COMPETITION
Wednesday 19 June 1996

Results

Foursomes Team	Score	
A. W. Kerr & Mrs R. Chorley	30	Winners
R. G. Halliday & S. Wilson	27	Runners - up
J. Cameron & Mrs J. Mann	26	3rd
I. Gram Hansen & Mrs M. Adams	26	4th

Other Scores

B. Eldred & Mrs A. McGlynn	25
R. Cunningham & Mrs S. Marsh	25
W. R. Allan & Mrs N. Milne	23
J. Train & R. Christie	23
H. Hanlon & Mrs E. Ramsay	23
E. Mackay & Mrs M. Connolly	22
R. Colman & Mrs L. Hutchison	21
N. Marsh & Mrs W. Schumacher	21
H. Connell & Mrs C. Miller	20
W. Chalmers & A. Masson	19
R. Adams & Mrs B. Smith	19
J. Bald & T. Chorley	18
W. Twaddle & W. Hay	18
W. B. Gray & Mrs J. Cunningham	18
J. W. Anderson & Mrs E. B. Mackay	17
W. B. Millar & W. Hutchison	17
J. Hunter & G. Brown	17
D. Sangster & Mrs K. Halliday	16
A. Wark & Mrs D. Andrews	15
J. Thomson & W. McRae	14
T. Ward & Miss B. Crichton	13
W. Cowie & Mrs C. Twaddle	n.r.

GENTS INVITATIONAL TEAM COMPETITION
Thursday 20 June 1996

INVITATIONAL RESULTS
(Best 3 scores out of 4)

CLUB	SCORE	
Pitreavie	205	Winners
Auchterderran	210	Runner up

Other Scores

Glenrothes	211	
Kinghorn	214	
Dunfermline	216	
Canmore	218	
Burntisland	219	
Edzell	219	
Balbirnie	229	
Dunnikier	252	

ABERDOUR RESULTS

Aberdour 2	197	Winners
(D. Ritchie, M. Dowling, W. Crowe, L. Wahlroos)		

Other Scores

Aberdour 4	203
Aberdour 6	210
Aberdour 5	211
Aberdour 1	211
Aberdour 3	212

SPONSORS DAY COMPETITION
TEXAS SCRAMBLE - Friday 21 June 1996

	COMPANY	ABERDOUR MEMBER	SCORE
1st	Castleblair	Hugh Hanlon	52.2
2nd	Pipe Industries Guild (2)	Jimmy Johnston	55.2
3rd	Edinburgh Fund Managers (2)	Stuart Meiklejohn	55.8

Other Scores

	Scottish Life (1)	Graham Milne	57.4
	Scottish Life (2)	Andrew Hubble	57.4
	Pipe Industries Guild (1)	Noel Marsh	58.2
	EDC Pipework Services (2)	Bill Millar	59.2
	Martin Bald Ltd	Bill Allan	59.2
	Flear & Thomson (1)	Alick Grant	59.4
	Hewlett Packard	Willie Crowe	60.2
	Edinburgh Fund Managers (1)	I Gram-Hansen	60.2
	Fortronic Ltd	Ben Eldred	60.6
	Royal Bank of Scotland	Alasdair Raffan	62.8
	Timbercraft	Ian McIntyre	64.1
	EDC Pipework Services (1)	Bob Pearston	64.2
	Flear & Thomson (2)	Mel Forrest	N.R.

CENTENARY CUP COMPETITIONS
Saturday 22 June 1996

GENTS

1st	W. Mackay	73	(16)	60	
2nd	I. Maxwell	80	(18)	62	
3rd	A. Parker	80	(16)	64	B.I.H.
4th	D. Miller	69	(5)	64	

LADIES

1st	M. Christie	90	(22)	68	
2nd	E. Rae	89	(19)	70	B.I.H.
3rd	S. Page	87	(17)	70	
4th	D. Cuthill	86	(15)	71	

JUNIORS
Played over 12 holes

1st	E. Crozier	56	(15)	41	Joint Winner
1st	D. McNeil	57	(16)	41	Joint Winner
3rd	A. Rae	64	(22)	42	
4th	P. Gordon	63	(19)	44	

TRI - AM COMPETITION
Sunday 11 August 1996

Winners - A. McGlynn, M. McGlynn, A. McGlynn

TEXAS SCRAMBLE
Sunday 18 August 1996

Winners - W. Heggie, W. Heggie, G. Heggie, P. Smith

CELEBRITY AM TOURNAMENT
Sunday 1 September 1996

1st	A.R.Hutt	A.Laing	S.Christie	Lindsay Hamilton, East Fife	119
2nd	P.White	M.Crawford	A.Kerr	Graham Everett, Athletics	121
3rd	H.Lavery, Sponsor	E.Key, Guest	S.Meiklejohn	Tom Callaghan, jnr, Football	124
4th	Rbt.Colman	W.McKay	A.McLaren	Ivo Den Bieman, Dunfermline	124
5th	P.Smith	N.McKay	P.Barton	Ben Gunn, Comedy	124

Other Scores

A.Parker, Sponsor	M.Redford, Guest	C.Gray	Davie Provan, Football	126
I.McIntyre	I.Mitchison	P.Coombes	Neville Taylor, Stars Org.	126
T.McIntyre	H.Thomson	P.McCann	Gordon McCallum, Golf Pro	126
O.Polland, Sponsor	G.Polland, Guest	Rosie Scott	Derek Lord, "Take the High Road"	128
J.McCulloch,Sponsor	D.McKee, Guest	P.Halleron	Ronnie Simpson, Football	128
W.Cross	M.Scott	R.Goodale	Brian Rice, Dunfermline Athletic	128
R.Aikman	D.Houston	S.Drever	Jim Brown, Football	129
Wtr Heggie	Ian Dewar, Tennis	John Robertson and	Darren Beckford, Hearts	130
J.Scott	S.Cowan	G.Taylor	Bobby Shearer, Football	131
M.Wood	I.Burns	W.Wood	Dick Campbell, Dunfermline	131
J.Wilson, Sponsor	E.Archibald, Guest	A.Hubble	Jim Law, Theatre	132
D.Levein	A.McGregor	J.MacDonald	Bert Allan, Comedy	182
I.Watt	W.Miller	E.Rae	Alan Soutar, Assist., Aberdour G.C.	132
I.MacDonald	Jean Bald	W.Heggie		132
A.Cruickshank	A.Thurogood	R.Maceachen	Colin Cameron, Hearts	132
J.Pearston	D.Cook, jnr	A.Ellington	Kevin Thomas, Hearts	133
R.Grant	S.Carnegie	M.Simpson	Jackie Farrell, "Take the High Road"	133
M.Izzi	T.Ward	I.Simpson	Mark Miller, Dunfermline	133
B.Kelly	S.Marsh	B.Munro	Peter Brown, Rugby	133
W.Fyffe	Les Wilson	L.Ross	Tom Callaghan, Snr, Football	133
N.Hill	S.Wilson	M.Christie	Ken Paton, Theatre	134
G.Heggie	Lois Wilson	K.Laming	Frank McGarvey, Football	134
M.Dowling, Sponsor	D.Murray, Guest	W.Twaddle	Richard Corsie, Bowls	135
D.Gault	T.Meakin	W.Bartley	John Blackley, Football	135
N.Milne	Jack Bald	M.Laing	Peter Morrison, Entertainment	136
A.Jess, Sponsor	T.Deacon, Guest	M.Forrest	Pat Clinton, Boxing	136
H.Hanlon	J.Milligan	T.Gray	Gordon Durie, Rangers	138
J.Horn, Sponsor	A.Wyles, Guest	W.Crowe	Joe Camay, Comedy	138
J.Johnston		Alec Howden, Comedy	Andy Tod, Dunfermline	139
B.Smith	E.B.Mackay	R.Wahlroos	Ally Logan, Entertainment	144

APPENDIX 10

TROPHIES FOR AMATEUR OPEN GOLF COMPETITIONS

THE ABERDOUR CUP
Purchased by the Club in 1973 and awarded annually to the competitor returning the best scratch score in the Aberdour Open Competition.

THE DRYBROUGH CUP
Donated to Aberdour Golf Club by Mr John Thorne of Drybrough Brewers and awarded annually to the competitor returning the lowest net score in the Aberdour Open Competition (Handicaps 1 to 12).

THE HAWKCRAIG TROPHY
Donated to Aberdour Golf Club by Mr William Fyffe of Brett Precision Components Limited and awarded annually to the competitor returning the lowest net score in the Aberdour Open Competition (Handicaps 13 to 25).

THE GRAM TROPHY
Donated to Aberdour Golf Club by I and Mrs M T Gram-Hansen and awarded annually to the competitor returning the lowest net score in the Aberdour Seniors' Open Competition.

THE CHARLES HAWKINS TROPHY
Donated to Aberdour Golf Club by Mr Rodney Hawkins in memory of his father and awarded annually to the Aberdour player returning the lowest net score in the Aberdour Seniors' Invitation Open Competition.

THE ROYAL BANK TROPHY
Donated to Aberdour Golf Club by The Royal Bank of Scotland and awarded annually to the competitor returning the lowest net score in the Ladies' Open Competition (Handicap limit 30).

THE ST ANDREWS BREEZE TROPHY
Donated to Aberdour Golf Club by Mrs Dorothy Andrews and awarded annually to the competitor returning the lowest net score in the Senior Ladies' Open Competition (Handicap limit 30).

THE J A GRAY QUAICH
Donated by Mr Jack Gray to Aberdour Golf Club and awarded annually to the competitor returning the lowest net score over 18 holes in the Aberdour Girls' Open Competition.

THE ST FILLANS TROPHY
Donated by Mrs Bunty Smith to Aberdour Golf Club and awarded annually to the competitor returning the lowest net score over 9 holes in the Aberdour Girls' Open Competition.

THE KYLE SALVER
Donated by Miss Sandra Wilson to Aberdour Golf Club and awarded annually to the Aberdour Competitor returning the lowest net score in the Aberdour Girls' Open Competition.

THE HI-FAS TROPHY
Donated by Mr John Quinn to Aberdour Golf Club and awarded annually to the competitor returning the lowest scratch score in the Aberdour Boys' Open Competition.

THE ROBERT PEARSTON CUP
Donated by Mr Robert Pearston to Aberdour Golf Club and awarded annually to the couple returning the lowest net score in the Aberdour Mixed Open Competition (Handicap limit L.33 -G.22).

THE FOULIS TROPHY
Donated by Mr Robert Foulis to Aberdour Golf Club and awarded annually to the couple returning the lowest net score in the Aberdour Invitation Greensomes Competition.

Centenary Bridge